The Presidential Libraries

The Herbert Hoover Library
West Branch, Iowa

The Franklin D. Roosevelt Library
Hyde Park, New York

The Harry S. Truman Library
Independence, Missouri

The Dwight D. Eisenhower Library
Abilene, Kansas

The John F. Kennedy Library
(Future Site) Cambridge, Massachusetts

The Lyndon B. Johnson Library
Austin, Texas

WHAT THE PRESIDENT OF THE UNITED STATES DOES

Roy Hoopes

The John Day Company
An Intext Publisher
New York

(Preceding page) The White House is both the home and the office of the president of the United States. It is also called the Executive Mansion. George Washington picked the site for the White House and approved James Hoban's design, which won the Irish architect and builder a five hundred dollar prize as well as a place in history. The first president to occupy the White House was John Adams, who moved into the still uncompleted North Wing in 1800, three years after George Washington left office. Thomas Jefferson was the first president to spend a full term in the White House. He was succeeded by James Madison in 1804, who served for two terms.

The British burned the White House during the War of 1812, and it was unoccupied during most of James Madison's second term. Since then, down through the years, numerous additions and changes have been made to the original building. The White House has become one of the most historic sites in the nation and is probably the country's most popular tourist attraction. More than a million and a half people visit the White House each year, passing through it on guided tours of its many historic rooms, while the president and his staff conduct the nation's business in adjoining offices. *(The White House)*

Copyright © 1974 by Roy Hoopes

Library of Congress Cataloging in Publication Data

Hoopes, Roy, 1922-
  What the President of the United States does.
  1. Presidents—United States.   2. United States—
Politics and government—20th century.   I. Title.
JK511.H65   353.03'13   74-5067
ISBN 0-381-99628-X   Reinforced Edition

The John Day Company, 257 Park Avenue South, New York, N.Y. 10010.

Published on the same day in Canada by Longman Canada Limited.

Printed in the United States of America.

4

ACKNOWLEDGMENTS

I wish to extend my appreciation to the directors and staffs of the six presidential libraries and to the Assistant Archivist for Presidential Libraries, Daniel J. Reed. The cooperation and assistance of the following people were especially helpful in the successful completion of this project:

The Herbert Hoover Library: Thomas Thalken, Director; Robert Wood, Assistant Director; J. Patrick Wildenberg, Audiovisual Archivist

The Franklin D. Roosevelt Library: the late J. C. James, Director; William J. Stewart, Assistant Director; Dr. James Whitehead, Curator

The Harry S Truman Library: Dr. B. K. Zobrist, Director; Philip D. Lagerquist, Chief Archivist; C. W. Ohrvall, Photo Archivist

The Dwight D. Eisenhower Library: John E. Wickman, Director; W. A. Scott, Staff Photographer; Don Wilson, Historian

The John F. Kennedy Library: Dan H. Fenn, Director; Alan Goodrich, Audiovisual Archivist; Joseph M. Tagariello, Archives Technician

The Lyndon B. Johnson Library: Harry Middleton, Director; Linda Wolfe, Still Photo Office

Finally, I am indebted to my wife, Cora, for her careful editing, and to my daughter, Sallie, for her assistance in preparation of the manuscript.

Books by Roy Hoopes

What the President of the United States Does
What a State Governor Does
What a Pro Football Coach Does
What a United States Congressman Does
What a Baseball Manager Does (with Spencer Hoopes)
What a United States Senator Does
What the President Does All Day
Getting With Politics
The Complete Peace Corps Guide
The Peace Corps Experience
The Steel Crisis
A Report on Fallout in Your Food
State Universities and Colleges
The High Fidelity Reader
Building Your Record Library
Wit From Overseas

*To the men and women
who operate
the country's
presidential
libraries.*

Presidential Photography

Photography did not develop in America until around 1839. The first president to have his photograph taken—a daguerreotype—was John Quincy Adams while he served in the House of Representatives, several years after he had left the White House. The first president to have his photograph taken while in office was John Tyler (1841–1845). On April 12, 1844, John Quincy Adams had a daguerreotype made in a Senate committee room, and he entered in his diary that, as he left the room, "President Tyler and his son, John, came in." Tyler's photograph was a part of a collection of daguerreotypes of famous Americans taken by Edward Anthony. Except for a single photograph of John Quincy Adams, this collection was destroyed by fire in 1952.

A daguerreotype of President Andrew Jackson was made at his home in Tennessee just before his death in 1845 by the famous Civil War photographer, Mathew Brady. Brady also made a daguerreotype of President Martin Van Buren after Van Buren left office, and the first photograph of a president, Zachary Taylor, and his Cabinet was made in 1849. Taylor died shortly after taking office and, in 1850, Brady made a photograph of Taylor's successor, Millard Fillmore.

Photographic coverage of our presidents improved every year as the art of photography developed. Today, there are several photographers on the regular White House staff. Each of the presidential libraries contains an extensive collection of photographs of the particular president whose life and career are documented in the library.

Many of the photographs in the presidential libraries are in the public domain and can be reproduced with permission from the library.

John Tyler (*Daguerreotype by Mathew Brady/Library of Congress*)

Martin van Buren (*Daguerreotype by Mathew Brady/Library of Congress*)

CONTENTS

1

THE PRESIDENCY
OF THE UNITED STATES

*The toughest and most powerful job in the
world was created by the Constitution—but
molded by men and events.*

The most famous address in the nation is 1600 Pennsylvania Avenue, N.W., Washington, D.C. It is the home and office of the president of the United States. As the leader of more than two hundred million people who make up the wealthiest and probably the most powerful nation in the world, the man who occupies the Oval Office of the President of the United States holds the most demanding, and possibly the most influential job in the world. From George Washington, our first president, until Richard M. Nixon, thirty-six men have held the office. We have had "strong" presidents, "weak" presidents and what some historians call "adequate" presidents. A few have emerged as truly great men;

others did not measure up to the responsibilities placed upon them. Taken collectively, though, these thirty-six men have given America remarkable leadership. They have guided her from her early beginnings as a sparsely populated group of thirteen essentially agricultural states on the Atlantic coast to what came to be called her "manifest destiny"— a powerful industrial nation of fifty states, spreading westward from the Atlantic to the Pacific and beyond. The role our presidents played in this development was best summed up by the nineteenth-century editor, Henry Jones Ford, who wrote: "The agency of the presidential office has been such a master force in shaping public policy that to give

(*continued on page 15*)

George Washington, on the balcony of the Federal Hall in New York City, taking the oath of office as the first president of the United States: "I do solemnly swear," he said, "that I will faithfully execute the Office of President of the United States and will, to the best of my ability, preserve, protect and defend the Constitution of the United States." A few minutes after the swearing-in ceremony, a procedure followed by every incoming president since Washington, he entered the Senate Chamber to deliver the nation's first inaugural address.

In it he set forth the objectives of his administration, which all presidents since Washington have done in their inaugural addresses. He also spoke of the "magnitude" of the job and his own "deficiencies" in preparing for the task ahead. But he was certain that "the experiment intrusted to the hands of the American people" would succeed if the people would always remember that "the propitious smiles of Heaven can never be expected on a nation that disregards the eternal rules of order and right which Heaven itself has ordained."

Eight years later, at the end of his second term, Washington prepared a message to the "people of the United States," which was printed in a Philadelphia newspaper. It was reprinted in dozens of newspapers in America and abroad and, eventually, became known as Washington's "Farewell Address." In it he warned his countrymen against the excesses of political parties, the dangers of involvement with foreign countries, and "to guard against the impostures of pretended patriotism."

As our first president, Washington firmly established the concept that the presidency is the dominant voice in the nation's foreign affairs. At home, however, he tended to be influenced more by the wishes of Congress and he relied heavily on the Cabinet system of government, which he conceived, to guide him in formulating domestic policies. (*Lithograph made from the original painting by Chappel/Library of Congress*)

Thomas Jefferson, president from 1801 to 1809, is remembered primarily for his concept of a great nation free of all forms of tyranny and injustice. He was cautious about exceeding the powers granted in the Constitution and generally viewed himself as the leader of his party and executor of the will and laws of Congress. However, he did not hesitate to use the powers of the office to contribute to the development and growth of the young country which he firmly believed would someday be one of the greatest in the world. For this reason, he purchased the Louisiana Territory from France without waiting for congressional authority. But he still felt the chief executive's powers should be restricted and, on completing his second term, he chose not to run for a third term on the grounds that it might turn the office into an "inheritance." This precedent, of limiting the president's term of office to two terms, lasted until the presidency of Franklin D. Roosevelt. Jefferson, unlike Washington, believed in political action through political parties and he is generally considered the founder of the Democratic party. *(Painting by Gilbert Stuart/Library of Congress)*

John Quincy Adams (1825–1829) had a long and distinguished career in the service of his country, as an ambassador, a U.S. senator, secretary of state, president and, in his final years, as a member of the House of Representatives. He served one term in the White House, and, although he was a forceful individual, Adams was not an especially strong president, primarily because of his view of the office. He refused to engage in the politics of his day and, as did many of our earlier presidents, felt that Congress and the courts were the most powerful branches of government.

He did, however, make one significant contribution to the concept of the presidency: he believed the office and its powers should be used to develop a great society. Adams felt that the reason God had endowed one nation with so many riches and natural resources was to produce a new and different civilization—rich, happy, wise and free from ignorance, poverty and disease. He hoped to achieve these goals by using the money from the sale of public lands to encourage the development of education and science in the country. "The great objective of the institution of civil government," Adams said in a message to Congress, "is the improvement of those who are partners to the social compact"—in other words, all the American people.

Adams was followed by Andrew Jackson, who had different ideas about how to use the powers of the presidency. Despite the fact that Adams served many years in public life after he left the presidency, he did not live long enough to see his vision of a great society translated into reality. But his approach to government and the presidency influenced many of our subsequent presidents. *(From a daguerreotype made in 1843 by P. Haas/Library of Congress)*

Andrew Jackson (1829–1837) firmly established the principle that, since the president was the choice of all the people, the presidency was just as strong and important as the other two branches of government. He was the first president to appeal directly to the people over the heads of their representatives in Congress. He won popular support by advocating that public lands be thrown open to the people and public offices should go primarily to presidential supporters. Jackson argued that not only did the president represent the American people, but, as one student of the presidency has pointed out, he felt that the president actually embodied the people. In his famous message to Congress, vetoing Henry Clay's bill to recharter the second Bank of the United States, Jackson set forth his view of the relationship between the three branches of government. "The Congress, the Executive and the Court," he said, "must each for itself be guided by its own opinion of the Constitution. Each public officer who takes an oath to support the Constitution swears that he will support it as he understands it, not as it is understood by others . . . The opinion of the judges has no more authority over Congress than the opinion of Congress has over the judges, and on that point the President is independent of both. . . ."

Jackson was called a tyrant by his opponents. He was accused by Henry Clay of fomenting a revolution that would result in the "concentration of all power in the hands of one man." He never did seize "all power," nor was that his intention. But, in his eight years in the White House, Jackson established the fact that the presidency when in the hands of a man not afraid to use its inherent powers, was the most powerful force in our government. *(India ink copy of an original daguerreotype made by Mathew Brady at Jackson's home in Tennessee shortly before his death in 1845/Library of Congress)*

James Polk (1845–1849) also presided in the tradition of presidents who did not hesitate to take strong action to accomplish things they felt were in the best interest of the nation. Polk risked war with England to acquire Oregon and involved the United States in an unpopular war with Mexico to acquire California. But in rounding out the continental shape of the nation, Polk felt he was doing what the people as a whole desired, even though critics in the Congress and the press felt that his action went beyond the powers granted him by the Constitution. Polk wrote in his diary: "The President represents in the executive department the whole people of the United States, as each member of the legislative department represents portions of them." As one historian points out, virtually every strong president since Polk repeated these words in one form or another. *(Library of Congress)*

13

The greatest test of the office of the presidency in relation to the Constitution came during the Civil War and the presidency of Abraham Lincoln (1861–1865). As chief executor of the laws of the United States, President Lincoln faced an insurrection against these laws when the Southern states seceded from the Union. And, as commander in chief of the armed forces, he was the ranking military leader in an actual theater of war when the Confederacy invaded the North. As one student of the presidency, Arthur Tourtellot, wrote, "hair-splitting" about his Constitutional powers probably would have lost the war for Lincoln and led to the permanent dissolution of the Union. But fortunately for the nation, Lincoln clearly saw the problem: "I did understand, however, that my oath to preserve the Constitution to the best of my ability impressed upon me the duty of preserving by every indispensable means, that government—that Nation of which the Constitution was the organic law. Was it possible to lose the Nation and yet preserve the Constitution?"

Lincoln decided it was and that as commander in chief of the armed forces in time of war he had authority to suspend the Constitution, if necessary, to save the nation. However, Lincoln realized that he was seizing extraordinary powers not granted in the Constitution and that no president could do this without overwhelming public support. "With public sentiment on its side," Lincoln said of the presidency, "everything succeeds, with public sentiment against it, nothing succeeds." (Below) President Lincoln meets with Union forces at Antietam, Maryland, October 3, 1862. General George McClellan, fourth man to Lincoln's right, is facing the president. (*Alexander Gardner/Library of Congress*)

a detailed account of it would be equivalent to writing the political history of the United States."

To be eligible to hold the office of president, a man must be at least thirty-five years old, a "natural born citizen" of the United States and a resident of this country for at least fourteen years. The term of office is for four years and the twenty-second Amendment to the Constitution limits him to two terms. He is elected by the people of the United States, but the actual election takes place through a process known as the Electoral College system.

The United States has three branches of government: the judiciary (the courts); the legislative (Congress) and the executive (the presidency). The men who drafted our Constitution intended that these three branches be equal and that no one branch would ever emerge permanently as the most powerful force in the government.

The duties and responsibilities of the president as set forth in Article II of the Constitution are surprisingly brief, considering the vast power of the office of the presidency today. The president is the commander in chief of the armed forces and, with the "advice and consent" of the Senate, has the power to make treaties. He appoints ambassadors, Supreme Court judges and all other officers of the United States not otherwise provided for in the Constitution. He has the power to grant reprieves and pardons and must "take care that the laws be officially executed." He must also give information to the Congress from time to time on the state of the union and recommend such "measures as he shall judge necessary and expedient." He can, on "extraordinary occasions," convene either or both houses of the Congress. However, to implement many of the things he is empowered to do, he must have money, and this can only be appropriated by the Congress.

In short, as many historians have pointed out, the framers of the Constitution were very cautious when they set forth the powers of the presidency. It is said that, anticipating George Washington would be the first president, they purposely left somewhat vague the section of the Constitution defining presidential powers. They expected George Washington to be a wise and strong president, thereby establishing precedents for later presidents to follow.

(continued on page 18)

Theodore Roosevelt in 1911. *(Library of Congress)*

Theodore Roosevelt (1901–1909) firmly believed in the concept of a "strong" presidency and, as a student of history and government, he knew that his actions in office would establish a precedent for future presidents. "I have felt," he said, "not merely my action was right in itself, but that in showing the strength of, or in giving strength to, the executive office, I was establishing a precedent of value."

The precedent Roosevelt wished to establish was that the president—when acting for the good of the people as a whole—could use any power not specifically denied him by the Constitution. "My belief," he said of the presidency, "was that it was not only his right but his duty to do anything that the needs of the Nation demanded unless such action was forbidden by the Constitution or by the laws. Under this interpretation of executive power, I did, and caused to be done, many things not previously done by the President and the heads of the Departments."

In domestic affairs, Roosevelt established the precedent, followed by many later presidents, of injecting the federal government into the economic affairs of the nation as a regulator of big business and as a creator of programs benefiting the nation as a whole. In foreign affairs, he believed the president should be even more powerful than at home. He virtually seized Panama, leaving Congress, as he said later in a speech, "to debate, and while the debate goes on, the canal does also."

However, Roosevelt understood, as Lincoln did, that to exercise such power a president must have the confidence of the people. Roosevelt had that confidence and he probably could have been elected to a third term. But instead of challenging the two-term precedent set by Washington and Jefferson, he decided to pick his successor—William Howard Taft.

Ironically, Taft (1909–1913) did not turn out to be as strong a president as Roosevelt expected, primarily because of Taft's interpretation of the Constitution. "While the President's powers are broad," Taft later wrote, "the lines of his jurisdiction are as fixed as a written Constitution can properly make them." Taft was a man of strong personal character, which reminds us that when historians appraise presidents as "strong" and "weak," the evaluation is based mostly on their interpretation of just how much power the Constitution grants the president—even when he judges his action to be for the good of all the people.

President William Howard Taft speaking at the courthouse in Manassas, Virginia, in 1911. *(Library of Congress)*

Woodrow Wilson (1913–1921) felt that the president was the only real voice in national affairs, and that only the president could speak and act for the whole nation. "A great nation," he said, "is not led by a man who simply repeats the talk of the street corners or the opinions of newspapers. A nation is led by a man who hears more than those things; who, rather, hearing those things, understands them better, unites them, puts them into a common meaning; speaks not the rumors of the street, but a new principle for a new age; a man [to whom] the voices of the nation . . . unite in a single meaning and reveal to him a single vision, so that he can speak what no one else knows, the common meaning of the common voice. . . ."

In his first term, Wilson was preoccupied with achieving governmental reforms, including the first graduated income tax and the creation of the Federal Reserve System. Shortly after his reelection in 1916, America entered World War I. Wilson guided the country through the war and, after it was over, risked his health in an effort to bring the United States into the League of Nations. However, a small group of senators managed to keep the United States out of the League, which left Wilson broken in spirit as well as in health. (Above) A tired President Wilson (left) rides in the back seat with President Warren G. Harding at Harding's inauguration in 1921. In the front seat is Senator Philander Knox (in top hat) and Speaker of the House of Representatives Joseph Cannon. *(Library of Congress)*

As it turned out, this is precisely what happened. The most significant precedent Washington established was the concept of a strong presidency. Down through the years, this encouraged other strong presidents to assume powers not specifically granted by the Constitution. Hence, the power the president exercises today rests as much on the political philosophy and achievements of past presidents as it does on Article II of the Constitution.

Having created a system in which power was divided equally among the three branches of government, it would have come as no surprise to the framers of the Constitution that, over the years, there would be periods in which one branch of government would become the most powerful, and then another. And that is the way it happened. In the years following George Washington's presidency, the Supreme Court and Congress played the most important role in leading the country. Then, beginning with President Andrew Jackson, the presidency became more powerful, culminating in the presidency of Abraham Lincoln, who exercised more power than any president up to that time, primarily because the office of the presidency was the only cohesive force in a nation torn by civil war.

After the Civil War, Congress again emerged as the most powerful of the three branches—until Theodore Roosevelt revived the concept of a strong president. Woodrow Wilson, and later Franklin D. Roosevelt, both presidents during world wars, and Roosevelt during the Great Depression, assumed even greater powers in guiding the nation through periods of crisis. As a result, it has been argued that the power of the presidency depends not only on the personality of the individual who holds the office, but on historical events. It is probably not coincidental that some of our "strongest" presidents —George Washington, Abraham Lincoln, Woodrow Wilson, and Franklin D. Roosevelt—occupied the presidency during periods of great national upheaval.

Historians feel that approximately one out of every three of our elected chief executives has been a "strong" president who has contributed to the growth of the office. Of course, when historians say a president is "strong" or "weak," they are usually referring to his interpretation of the Constitution and to what extent he feels he should assume the powers inherent in the presidency. Many of our so-called "weak" presidents were men who felt that when the country was not facing an emergency and the people were enjoying relatively good times, the president and the federal government should interfere as little as possible in the affairs of the nation.

History has shown that there is no way of telling who will make a great or a strong president and who will not. As presidential historian Sidney Hyman has written: ". . . Lincoln was unfit for everything except the Presidency, while a man like James Madison was unfit for the Presidency but magnificently fit for everything else." And James Polk entered the presidency with no reputation as a leader, and went into our history books as "one of the very best and most honest and most successful Presidents the country ever had," as historian George Bancroft put it.

Before he left office a tired and broken man, Woodrow Wilson had found that there were limits to the powers of the presidency. But in an earlier day, while he was still a Princeton professor, he wrote: "The President is at liberty, both in law and in conscience, to be as big a man as he can. . . ." Most students of government agree that this is still a good assessment of the presidency of the United States.

2

SIX PRESIDENTS

What is it like to be president of the United States, to hold the most difficult, exciting, and demanding job in the nation? Most presidents have agreed with President John F. Kennedy who said that no one can "realize who does not bear the burden of this office how heavy and constant" the burden is.

Through photographs and text, including the words of the presidents themselves, this book will try to show what it is like to hold the office of the presidency and the heavy burden it places on the man who holds it.

The focus will be on the last six presidents who are no longer in office: Herbert Hoover, Franklin D. Roosevelt, Harry S. Truman, Dwight D. Eisenhower, John F. Kennedy and Lyndon B. Johnson. All are dead, which is unusual. For most of our history the nation has had one or more living ex-

presidents to whom it could turn for advice and counsel. The complete record of each of these men now lies embodied in the presidential libraries that have been established in their honor in various locations around the country, but judgment on their performance in office will probably be reassessed by each new generation of historians.

Four of these presidents were Democrats and two were Republicans. While they were in the White House, however, each one tried to rise above partisan politics and serve all of the people. Individual presidents bring different policies, objectives and styles to the office, but every president is conscious of the fact that the presidency is a continuing office with a strength and identity above and beyond the conflicts of the day.

In a historic photograph, four of the six presidents to be considered in this book are shown together—at the funeral of the late Speaker of the House of Representatives, Sam Rayburn, in Bonham, Texas, November 18, 1961. (Left to right) John F. Kennedy, Lyndon B. Johnson, Dwight D. Eisenhower and Harry S. Truman. *(Wide World Photos)*

HERBERT HOOVER (1929–1933)

HERBERT HOOVER

Herbert Hoover, a Republican, will always be remembered as the president who had to face the 1929 stock market crash and the beginnings of the Great Depression of the 1930s in America and Europe.

To bring about economic recovery, Hoover encouraged voluntary remedies on the part of industry and the people. But at the same time he launched a federal recovery program that included the Federal Farm Board, Home Loan Banks and the Reconstruction Finance Corporation. Although Hoover was not afraid to use the powers of the presidency to achieve national goals, he was cautious about committing the federal government and its resources to combatting the Depression. "It is not the function of government," he said, "to relieve individuals of their responsibilities to their neighbors, or to relieve private institutions of their responsibilities to the public." However, he promoted the most extensive private relief efforts and the greatest public works program initiated by any president up until that time.

Although Hoover had been a highly successful and idealistic businessman and was a man of great personal strength and character, his leadership failed to bring about economic recovery. As a result the people, impatiently looking to the federal government for a speedy recovery, turned against their president. Hoover left the White House after the 1932 elections as one of the most unpopular presidents in American history. Some historians have taken the position that he did not act quickly enough or as extensively as he could have to achieve economic recovery. However, beginning in the 1950s, a re-evaluation of Hoover's presidency was begun, and historians now give Hoover more credit for his efforts to stave off the Depression and his vision in foreseeing some of the problems that would inevitably grow out of government intervention in the affairs of the people.

FRANKLIN D. ROOSEVELT

Franklin Delano Roosevelt was nominated as the Democratic presidential candidate in 1932, at a time when the people were so disappointed with Herbert Hoover that, according to Roosevelt's campaign manager, it would have been impossible for any Democrat *not* to be elected.

Roosevelt felt that in order to achieve economic recovery it was essential for the people to regain faith in themselves. He also realized that recovery was not possible without massive federal programs designed to help the impoverished one-third of the nation. In the first 100 days of his new administration, Roosevelt helped push through the Congress fifteen major pieces of legislation. This was the foundation for his economic recovery programs, which became known as the "New Deal." Roosevelt's program also became the cornerstone of what critics of the New Deal later referred to as the "welfare state"—a broad social and economic program that called for controlling and adequately taxing industry, and using the money to help the poor, the unemployed, the uneducated, the ill and the handicapped. As the nation gradually began to regain its economic prosperity, businessmen and the well-to-do slowly turned against Roosevelt and his economic programs because they felt he was leading the country down the road to socialism. But he

FRANKLIN D. ROOSEVELT (1933–1945)

remained popular with the vast majority of the American people.

In 1936, he defeated the Republican candidate, Alfred Landon, in a landslide victory, with Roosevelt carrying all the states except Maine and Vermont. And in 1940, even though his popularity had slipped and he annoyed some people by defying tradition in running for a third term, he easily defeated the popular Republican Wendell Willkie.

One of Roosevelt's problems in trying to achieve his objectives was that the Supreme Court declared many of his acts unconstitutional. Roosevelt charged that the Court had laid a "dead hand" on his economic recovery program, preventing it from operating properly. After his landslide second-term election, Roosevelt announced a plan to enlarge the Supreme Court from nine to fifteen members. The proposal aroused strong opposition throughout the country and in his own party. Although it was defeated, Roosevelt achieved the same results, in later years, by appointing seven "liberals" to the Court as the older members died or retired.

In the course of his second term, Roosevelt was faced with other problems. Labor had organized and become more powerful, especially through the use of "sit-down" strikes, which infuriated private industry and angered many Americans. Roosevelt was caught in the middle, and during one strike he shocked both industry and labor by announcing, "A plague on both your houses." There was still considerable unemployment and business stagnation. "I see one-third of a Nation ill-housed, ill-clad and ill-nourished," he said in his second inaugural address. Criticism of Roosevelt's policies continued to mount, both from private industry, who said he was interfering too much in their affairs, and from the private citizens who said he was not doing enough.

When the war broke out in Europe in 1939 between Great Britain, France and Russia and the Fascist countries, Germany and Italy, although he was under great pressure to keep America neutral, Roosevelt gradually was drawn to the side of the Allies. Finally, the attack by Japan on Pearl Harbor on December 7, 1941, brought the United States into the war against Japan, Germany and

Italy. The stimulation of wartime production revived the American economy and Roosevelt was free to devote most of his third term to the problems of winning the war.

In 1944, Roosevelt, as a wartime president, was the overwhelming choice as the Democratic presidential candidate for an unprecedented fourth term, and Roosevelt decided to run again. At the Democratic convention, because of opposition to Vice-President Henry Wallace, Roosevelt dropped Wallace from the ticket and replaced him with a little-known senator from Missouri—Harry S. Truman. Roosevelt defeated Governor Thomas Dewey of New York, but on April 12, 1945, barely into his fourth term, he died at his "summer White House" in Warm Springs, Georgia. Roosevelt had been in office longer than any president in history, and his death came as a stunning shock to the American people who were looking for him to lead them to final victory and into the postwar world.

HARRY S. TRUMAN (1945–1953)

HARRY S. TRUMAN

No vice-president in the nation's history had ever been thrust so abruptly into a most difficult and demanding job—which he genuinely did not want —as Harry S. Truman. When President Roosevelt died in 1945, Truman told the reporters the next day, "I felt like the moon, the stars and all the planets had fallen on me."

Shortly after he assumed the presidency, Truman had to preside over America's entry into the United Nations at the San Francisco Conference. Later in 1945, he attended the historic Potsdam Conference where Allied powers discussed the postwar world and issued an ultimatum to Japan to surrender. When Japan refused, Truman decided to use the atomic bomb against Japan—at Hiroshima and Nagasaki—which brought an end to the war in the Pacific.

At home, Truman continued the Roosevelt economic and social programs designed to aid the underprivileged, stimulate the economy, protect the working man and regulate big business. Truman also presented the Congress with a domestic program of his own, known as the "Fair Deal." In 1946, the Republicans scored impressive victories in the congressional elections, and the Eightieth Congress,

which convened in January 1947, was controlled by the Republicans. The Eightieth Congress not only failed to act on most of Truman's Fair Deal programs, but enacted bills, over presidential veto, including the Taft–Hartley Act, which restricted labor union activities.

As the 1948 election approached, it was assumed that Truman would be easily defeated by his Republican opponent, New York Governor Thomas Dewey. Although the polls continued to declare Dewey the victor right up until election night, Truman waged—from the back platform of a railroad train—a tough "give-'em-hell" campaign, directed mostly at the "do nothing" Republican Eightieth Congress. On election night, he went to bed having heard radio commentator H. V. Kaltenborn announce his defeat. But next morning, when all the returns were in, Truman was still president, to the humiliation of the nation's "political experts."

Truman's presidency was marked by his struggle to resist Communist aggression abroad, which began in his first term. In 1947, when Russia threatened Greece and Turkey, Truman came to the defense of the two countries with economic and military aid. Later, this aid extended to all of Europe, came to be known as the Marshall Plan, named after Truman's Secretary of State, George C. Marshall.

In 1948, Truman countered a Russian blockade of Berlin with an airlift of supplies into Berlin's western zone, and the following year the United States was the guiding force in developing the North Atlantic Treaty Organization, a military alliance for the protection of western non-Communist nations. In 1950 when the United States learned that Russia had developed the atomic bomb, and Truman responded by going ahead with the development of the hydrogen bomb, the Cold War intensified. It finally became a shooting war in 1950, when the North Korean Communists invaded South Korea and President Truman and Secretary of State Dean Acheson rallied the United Nations to the defense of South Korea. The war lasted three years, and Truman's main challenge was to contain the war within the boundaries of Korea. This led to political difficulties with advocates of a more aggressive policy who were willing to risk a major war with China or Russia. They included General Douglas MacArthur, commander of United Nations forces in Korea, whose defiance of the president became so obvious that Truman was forced to fire him.

Although eligible to run for president again in 1952, Truman announced that he would not seek what he called a "third term," a decision, he said, he had made as early as 1949. "In my opinion," he wrote, "eight years as President is enough and sometimes too much for any man to serve in that capacity." Truman had not served a full eight years, but he considered the term in which he succeeded Franklin Roosevelt a full term. Truman's first choice as his successor was Supreme Court Justice Fred Vinson. But when Vinson declined to run, Truman shifted his support to Illinois Governor Adlai Stevenson, who eventually campaigned against General Dwight D. Eisenhower—and lost.

DWIGHT D. EISENHOWER

General Dwight D. Eisenhower defeated Illinois Governor Adlai Stevenson in 1952 and became the first Republican president since Herbert Hoover. After twenty years of the New and Fair Deal programs of Democratic presidents Roosevelt and Tru-

(George Tames)

DWIGHT D. EISENHOWER (1953–1961)

man, people apparently agreed with the 1952 Republican campaign slogan that it was "time for a change." With the hardships of the Great Depression forgotten, what concerned people most, after three years of frustrating warfare in Korea, was the threat of World War III. General Eisenhower, the hero of World War II, who had dedicated himself to keeping America strong in order to maintain United States leadership in the world, seemed the ideal man to preserve world peace.

"Ike," as he was called, did not let them down. Within six months after he took office, Eisenhower kept his campaign promise and brought the war in Korea to an end. He also worked tirelessly to ease the tensions in the Cold War with Russia. With both great powers having developed the potentially devastating hydrogen bomb, an arms control agreement seemed imperative. And after the death of Russian leader Joseph Stalin in 1953, there was hope that the new leaders in Russia would be agreeable to discussing a nuclear-arms agreement with the new leaders in America. At the United Nations, in his "Atoms for Peace" plan, and at the Geneva Conference in 1955, attended by leaders of France, Great Britain, Russia and the United States, Eisenhower kept pressing for a nuclear-arms agreement, and although little progress was made, the president eventually was able to relax tensions between Russia and the United States.

At home, Eisenhower disappointed the more conservative Republicans who had supported him by continuing most of the social welfare programs that had been initiated by Roosevelt and Truman. He was, however, increasingly concerned about the cost of these programs, and many of them were cut back somewhat in an effort to achieve a balanced budget. The movement for the complete desegregation of the blacks accelerated during the Eisenhower administration, after the 1954 Supreme Court decision declared segregation unconstitutional. Eisenhower sent federal troops to Little Rock, Arkansas, in 1954 to back up a federal court order calling for the desegregation of schools. He also took the leadership in the desegregation of the Armed Forces and signed the first civil rights legislation to pass the Congress since 1875.

Although the beginnings of the civil rights movement and the lingering cold war with Russia produced some tensions at home and abroad, the first four years of the Eisenhower administration were years of peace and prosperity in America, and Ike continued to be one of the most popular men ever to occupy the White House. And despite the fact that he had a heart attack in 1955, an intestinal operation in 1956 and faced increasing opposition from the "Old Guard" conservative wing of his party, Ike was easily the overwhelming choice of Republicans to lead them in 1956. He kept Vice-President Nixon as his running mate and his Democratic opponent, again, was Adlai Stevenson. In a campaign dominated by the issue of testing hydrogen bombs, which were releasing lethal strontium–90 in the atmosphere, Eisenhower buried Stevenson in a landslide. However, the Congress, which had gone Republican in 1952 and Democratic in 1954, remained Democratic.

Eisenhower considered his landslide victory as a mandate for his program of "dynamic conservatism," which was marked by the continuation of the Democratic social welfare programs but with more attention given to the national budget and the interests of big business. In general, the country's peace and prosperity and its affection for President Eisenhower continued through most of his second term. But as 1960 approached, Eisenhower received more and more criticism from the Republican Old Guard for his failure to turn back the New and Fair Deal programs, and from an increasing number of critics who charged that he was spending too little time in the White House.

Abroad, the threat of war in the Middle East, the failure of the United States to support the Hungarians when they revolted against Russia, the shooting down of a U.S. reconnaissance plane by the Russians, the breaking off of diplomatic relations with Red China, the apparent lagging behind the Soviets—as symbolized by Russia's launching of the world's first earth satellite—and the continuing failure to reach a nuclear-arms agreement with Russia, all combined to dampen Eisenhower's image as an invincible world leader.

Nevertheless, it is generally agreed that were it not for the two-term limitation imposed by the Twenty-second Amendment, Ike would have been the Republican nominee for president again in 1960, and would have easily defeated any Democratic opponent. However, his popularity was not enough to help Vice-President Richard Nixon, the Republican candidate, win the presidency.

In one of his last speeches, President Eisenhower warned that America must be continually alert to the problems presented by the combination of a large military force, ever expanding because of the Cold War, and the powerful military arms industry, which needed war and international tension for its continuing prosperity. Coming from one of the nation's greatest military heroes, it is a speech that is still being widely quoted.

JOHN F. KENNEDY

John F. Kennedy was the youngest man, and the first Roman Catholic, ever to be elected president. He was assassinated on November 22, 1963, as he rode in a presidential motorcade through the streets of Dallas, Texas, before he had completed three full years in office. Although we will never have a full measure of Kennedy as a president, we know

(The White House)

JOHN F. KENNEDY (1961–1963)

problems of peace and war, unconquered pockets of ignorance and prejudice, unanswered questions of poverty and surplus." Later, in his inaugural address, he indicated that he intended to bring a new vigor to the presidency and the nation when he said "a new generation of Americans" had taken over the nation's destiny. And he urged all Americans to "ask not what your country can do for you —ask what you can do for your country."

Kennedy was in the White House long enough to reveal the direction he wanted the nation to take at home and abroad. His legislation submitted to Congress was designed to carry on the liberal, Democratic tradition of enlisting the federal government in the fight against man's ancient enemies, ignorance, disease and poverty. His proposals included legislation to help the farmers, provide aid to educational institutions, assist the elderly with medical problems, reform the tax structure, stimulate economic growth, assure civil rights for black Americans, rehabilitate depressed areas and curb unemployment. John Kennedy's inclination to side with the average citizen against big business was dramatized in his confrontation with the steel industry. He forced the companies to reverse their decision to raise steel prices because he feared it would start another round of price rises throughout the entire economy.

In his short period in the presidency, Kennedy amply demonstrated the dimensions of his foreign policy: international cooperation, a firm stand against the Communist expansion, and a generous program to help underprivileged nations fight the conditions of poverty that breed social unrest. After the Bay of Pigs disaster, an unsuccessful effort— planned before he took office—to overthrow the Cuban Communist leader Fidel Castro, Kennedy launched a ten-year Alliance for Progress program designed to prevent the spread of Communism in Latin America. He also responded to the idealistic beliefs of the youth of America in the early 1960s by creating the Peace Corps, which encouraged and trained young people to serve in the underdeveloped nations of the world. And he responded to increased Russian military pressures on Berlin and the resumption of nuclear-weapons testing by the Soviets by requesting Congress to increase American military preparedness and by resuming U.S. nuclear tests. When it was learned that Russian Premier

from his three years in the White House that he had the potential for greatness. Not only did he advance lofty goals for the nation, he had the ability to inspire others. He made mistakes, such as the ill-conceived Bay of Pigs operation against Cuban dictator Fidel Castro, but he also proved to be a decisive leader when he rallied the nation to stand firm against the Russians, during the Cuban missile crisis.

Although the nation needed the eight years of Eisenhower's "peace and prosperity" while it recovered from the upheaval of the Roosevelt economic revolution, World War II and the discovery of nuclear energy, in 1960, Kennedy felt that it was time for America to move into a new age. "We stand today on the edge of a New Frontier," he said in his acceptance speech at the Democratic Convention in Los Angeles. "Beyond that frontier are uncharted areas of science and space, unsolved

Nikita Khrushchev was installing missile bases in Cuba capable of firing nuclear weapons close range at the United States, President Kennedy made a dramatic television address proclaiming a U.S. "quarantine" on all weapons being sent to Cuba, and demanded that Khrushchev halt construction of the Cuban missile bases. After a week of international tension, in which many people felt Russia and the United States were on the brink of nuclear war, Khrushchev finally backed down. Subsequent to the missile crisis, Kennedy tried to move the country closer to international cooperation with Russia through a limited arms-control agreement.

Kennedy did not live to see the results of his foreign policy, and one of the questions historians will ponder is whether he would have let the nation become more deeply involved in Vietnam. Nor did he live long enough to see the Apollo missions to the moon climax a space program launched by Congress during his administration. But despite the briefness of his moment in history, people will always remember President Kennedy and his attractive family for the excitement and high purpose that they brought to the White House.

LYNDON B. JOHNSON (1963–1969)

(The White House)

LYNDON B. JOHNSON

Lyndon B. Johnson, the thirty-sixth president of the United States, entered the White House under tragic circumstances, comparable perhaps only to President Andrew Johnson's assumption of the presidency. Two hours after John F. Kennedy was hit by bullets, Lyndon Johnson was sworn in as president on *Air Force One* at the Dallas airport. When he returned to Washington he told the nation: "I will do my best. That is all I can do." Later he urged: "All my fellow Americans, let us continue"—which became the underlying theme of Johnson's first year in office.

Historians agree that President Johnson managed the sudden transition from the Kennedy to the Johnson administration with tact and skill. In the first Johnson years, many Kennedy programs that had been stalled in Congress were enacted. Kennedy's policies were continued, and Kennedy's men were asked to stay in the administration for as long as they wished. Some stayed on through Johnson's

entire administration. In the 1964 presidential elections, Johnson was challenged by the Republican conservative Senator Barry Goldwater. The outcome was one of the biggest landslides in American history. Johnson and his running mate, Senator Hubert Humphrey, won by a margin of fifteen million votes. The landslide also brought in the overwhelmingly liberal Democratic Eighty-ninth Congress. Johnson, feeling that he was now president in his own right, launched a vast legislative program to create what he called a "Great Society." Johnson also declared a "war on poverty" to accompany the dramatic programs in civil and, especially, voting rights for blacks, which had been recently initiated. The Eighty-ninth Congress responded with a flood of social legislation in the fields of health, education, welfare, housing and urban renewal—almost, some said, too much for the nation to absorb in such a short period of time.

Under President Johnson, America also accelerated its space program. In December 1968, Astronauts Frank Borman, James Lovell and William Anders became the first men to enter lunar orbit, a feat that paved the way for man's landing on the moon.

However, in foreign affairs, President Johnson and America became involved in one of the most difficult and complex situations in the nation's history. In an effort to prevent the little country of South Vietnam (which had been separated from North Vietnam by the 1954 Geneva convention) from being taken over by the Communists, the United States had been sending aid and advisers to South Vietnam since the presidency of General Eisenhower. This assistance was increased under President Johnson until, finally, the United States was involved in a major land war in Southeast Asia. Much of the nation, and especially America's youth, gradually became disenchanted with the war. By 1968, the country experienced not only antiwar demonstrations on the nation's campuses, but nationwide unrest led by blacks protesting against conditions in the ghettoes. With most of the nation's discontent focused on the president, as it usually is in a time of national unrest, Johnson chose not to run for the presidency again. He decided this was the best thing he could do to ease the tension, a decision he announced in a dramatic television broadcast on March 31, 1968. In an effort to bring about peace negotiations with the North Vietnamese Communists, he also announced that the United States was halting the bombing of North Vietnam. Vice President Hubert Humphrey became the Democratic presidential candidate, but was defeated by Richard Nixon in an election in which the war in Vietnam was a major issue. Nixon promised to end the war, a pledge he finally fulfilled four years later.

3
THE ROAD TO
THE WHITE HOUSE

One of our nation's oldest traditions is that any American child can grow up to become president of the United States. This is true. But the road to the White House is a long, hard, tiring one and any person who decides to take it will eventually be called "ambitious" and accused of having "White House fever."

Furthermore, just wanting to be president, or having the ability, is not enough. Before being considered "presidential timber," the prospective candidate must have a distinguished record of public service or be a national figure. For a while, being governor of a large state was the most promising route to the White House. But in recent years, with our increasing concern with international affairs, a distinguished career in the Senate of the United States proved to be a better springboard.

Of our six presidents, Roosevelt, Truman, Kennedy and Johnson came to the White House through the normal political process—Roosevelt as a governor, the others after serving in Congress. Truman and Johnson probably could not have won their party's nomination; each one entered the White House after the death of a president who had chosen them as vice-president. However, once in office, both won their party's nomination on their own and were elected president. Hoover and Eisenhower were not politicians but achieved na-

tional recognition in other fields—Hoover in business and public service and Eisenhower as a general in World War II.

At what point in life does a person decide he wants to be president? This is a hard question to answer. But studying the early careers of these six men who eventually became president gives us some understanding of how a man gets on the road to the White House.

HERBERT HOOVER: EARLY CAREER

Herbert Hoover was born in West Branch, Iowa, in 1874. His parents died while he was still a child, and he was raised by two uncles. He attended Quaker schools in Oregon, but at the same time held several part-time jobs. At fourteen, he went to work as an office boy, where he learned to type. He also took bookkeeping and mathematics at night school and became interested in mining. This led him to enroll in Stanford University. He worked his way through college, operating a newspaper route and a laundry agency and doing clerical work in the department of geology.

Hoover received his degree in 1895 and four years later married Lou Henry, a former student at Stanford. By 1908 he owned his own engineering firm, and at the beginning of World War I he was the managing director or chief consulting engineer for a number of mining companies all over the world. He was in Europe at the outbreak of the war and, after achieving recognition for his role in helping Americans return to the United States, he organized the Commission for Relief of Belgium, which fed that nation during the war. Later, he returned to America where President Woodrow Wilson made him a member of his "war cabinet" as U.S. Food Administrator. After the armistice, Wilson sent him back to Europe as director of the American Relief Mission. He also attended the Versailles Peace Conference as director of European Relief.

Hoover's stature as a public figure was such that in 1920 he was seriously considered by both parties for the presidential nomination. Hoover, James M. Cox and Warren G. Harding were the final choices, and after the Republican victory in 1920, Hoover was made secretary of commerce. He served in this

As Administrator of American Relief to Europe, Herbert Hoover returns from a trip to Europe in 1919 on board the S. S. *Aquitania*. *(New York Herald-Tribune/The Herbert Hoover Library)*

post during the Harding and Coolidge administrations with such distinction that by 1928 he was the obvious choice for the Republican nomination. During the campaign, he said that since the world was on the threshold of the greatest era of commercial expansion in history, he hoped to see the day when "poverty would be banished from this Nation." Hoover was easily elected president—by the greatest majority of any president prior to 1928.

FRANKLIN D. ROOSEVELT: EARLY CAREER

Franklin Roosevelt was born in 1882. His father was James Roosevelt, president of the Louisville, Albany and Chicago railroad, and Franklin was a distant cousin of Theodore Roosevelt, soon to become president of the United States. Roosevelt attended Groton, Harvard and Columbia University Law School. In 1905, while at Columbia, he married Anna Eleanor Roosevelt, daughter of

Senator John Kennedy campaigning in New Haven, Connecticut, in the 1960 campaign. *(The John F. Kennedy Library)*

New York Governor Roosevelt receives news of his reelection, November 4, 1930. *(The Franklin D. Roosevelt Library)*

election, Roosevelt was elected governor. He was reelected in 1930, and by 1932 was one of the most popular and highly respected Democrats in the country. Although he had to walk on crutches and spent most of his time in a wheelchair, he was nominated for the presidency at the Democratic convention in 1932 and defeated Herbert Hoover, becoming the thirty-second president of the country.

HARRY S. TRUMAN: EARLY CAREER

Harry S. Truman was born in 1884 in Lamar, Missouri, but grew up on a farm near Grandview. He attended local schools and was an excellent student, especially of history. He wanted to go to West Point, but was rejected because of poor vision. Truman spent his early manhood as a farmer on the family farm and was active in the National Guard. He was thirty-three when America entered World War I, but he immediately enlisted in the army and, as a result of his national guard duties, was made a first lieutenant. He was trained at the field artillery school at Fort Sill, Oklahoma, and was sent overseas as a captain in the Thirty-fifth Division. Having distinguished himself as the head of a field artillery battery, after the war he was discharged from the army as a captain in the reserves. Seven weeks after his discharge, Truman married Bess Wallace whom he had known since boyhood. He started a clothing store in Kansas City with a friend, Eddie Jacobson, but it failed in 1921. He also had become active in politics and, in 1922, was elected a judge of the Jackson County Court. This was an administrative job, not a legal one. Nevertheless, for two years Truman studied law at night school in Kansas City, but did not obtain his law degree. In 1934, with the support of a political boss, Tom Pendergast, he decided to run for the U.S. Senate. He won an impressive victory and went to Washington where he built a reputation as an honest, quiet and hard-working public official. He was reelected to the Senate in 1940. The turning point in Truman's career came in 1941, when he was appointed head of a special Senate committee created to investigate the performance of government agencies and private industries responsible for materials and services needed in the war. The Truman Committee, as it was known, became

Theodore Roosevelt's brother. The ceremony was attended by Theodore Roosevelt, who was president at that time, thereby diverting attention away from the bride and groom.

After leaving school, Roosevelt began to practice law, and later went into politics by winning election to the New York State Senate, where he served two terms. In 1912, he worked to help nominate and elect Woodrow Wilson and was rewarded for his loyalty by being appointed Assistant Secretary of the Navy, a post he still held when America entered World War I. After the war, in 1920, he went back into politics as the running mate of the presidential candidate James M. Cox. They were defeated and Roosevelt became a vice-president in the New York office of the Fidelity and Deposit Company of Maryland. In 1921, he was stricken with polio while vacationing at Campobello, Maine. The illness left him crippled for the rest of his life.

In 1924 and 1928, he helped New York Governor Al Smith in his efforts to win the presidency. In 1928, when Smith won the Democratic nomination he, in turn, urged Roosevelt to run for governor of New York. Although Smith lost the presidential

Senator Harry Truman on the steps of the U.S. Capitol, a few months before he became famous as head of the Senate's Truman Committee. *(Kansas City Journal)*

famous throughout the land for eliminating waste and corruption in defense contracts. The Committee is believed to have saved as much as fifteen billion dollars through its investigations, and Senator Harry Truman became a national figure.

At the 1944 Democratic convention, when opposition to Roosevelt's vice-president, Henry Wallace, developed, Roosevelt asked Truman to be his running mate. Truman did not want the job, but Roosevelt said that if Truman refused there would probably be a split in the party. He agreed to run as vice-president and the Roosevelt–Truman ticket won. A few months after the election, Franklin Roosevelt died suddenly, and Truman became president.

DWIGHT D. EISENHOWER: EARLY CAREER

Dwight D. Eisenhower was born in Denison, Texas, in 1890, but he spent his childhood in Abilene, Kansas. "Ike," as he was known in school,

graduated from high school in 1909 and, two years later, obtained an appointment to the military academy at West Point. This was the beginning of a long and successful career in the U.S. Army. In 1916, the day he was promoted to first lieutenant, Eisenhower married Mamie Doud. Their first son died; their second son, John, born in 1922, had four children: Dwight David II (who married Julie Nixon), Barbara Anne, Susan Elaine and Mary Jean.

By the time America entered World War II in 1941, Eisenhower was a general with a distinguished record. In 1942, he was appointed U.S. Commanding General in Europe, then Commander in Chief of Allied Forces, in charge of the Allied invasion of North Africa. Later, he commanded the invasion of Sicily and the invasion of Italy before being put in Supreme Command of the Allied Forces that landed at Normandy and, with the Russians, eventually defeated Germany.

When "Ike" returned to the United States after World War II, he was one of the most popular military heroes in American history. Almost immediately, pressure was put on him by both the Democrats and the Republicans to run for the presidency, but he refused. In 1948, the same year

General Eisenhower, as commander of the United States troops in Europe, watches Allied landing operations from the deck of a warship off the coast of France, June 7, 1944. *(The Dwight D. Eisenhower Library)*

of publication of his best-selling book about the war, *Crusade in Europe,* Eisenhower resigned from the Army to become president of Columbia University. He returned to the Army in 1950 and later was chosen by Truman to head the western military forces in Europe under the NATO command. In 1952, a presidential election year, the political leaders of both parties visited Ike at his headquarters in Paris and again tried to persuade him to run for the presidency. This time he agreed, primarily because of his interest in preserving peace and in making certain that America would maintain its leadership in world affairs. Considering himself a conservative in economic and domestic affairs, Ike chose to run as a Republican. In early summer of 1952, he came home to campaign in the primaries against Senator Robert Taft of Ohio. At the Republican convention, Ike was nominated on the first ballot. With Senator Richard Nixon as his vice-presidential candidate, Ike defeated his Democratic opponent, Adlai Stevenson, in a campaign in which he and Nixon promised to clean up the "mess in Washington" after twenty years of Democratic rule.

JOHN F. KENNEDY: EARLY CAREER

John F. Kennedy spent part of his childhood in Brookline, Massachusetts, where he was born in 1917, part in the New York City area, where his family took up residence in 1926, and most of his summers at the family home in Hyannisport on Cape Cod.

His father, Joseph P. Kennedy, was President Franklin Roosevelt's first chairman of the Securities and Exchange Commission and, later, U.S. Ambassador to Great Britain; so young Kennedy was exposed early to politics and public life. He attended, briefly, both the London School of Economics and Princeton before he entered Harvard in 1936. He graduated with honors from Harvard in 1940, also, having won with his brother, Joseph, the intercollegiate sailboat championship. He starred on the swimming team and worked on the editorial staff of the *Harvard Crimson.* Despite his slight build, he went out for the football team and, in his sophomore year, suffered a back injury in scrimmage that would trouble him for the rest of his life.

Senator Kennedy campaigning for the presidency in 1960. *(The Democratic Digest)*

In 1941, he enlisted in the Navy and was assigned to a Motor Torpedo Boat squadron in the Pacific. His PT–109 was rammed by the Japanese off the Solomon Islands in 1943. In rescue efforts to save his crewmen, he aggravated his back injury and was sent back to a Massachusetts naval hospital for treatment. While the future president was recuperating from back surgery, his older brother, Joe, was killed overseas. This event may have marked the turning point in John Kennedy's life. In the family, Joe had always been the one most interested in a public career, and after his death John felt that perhaps he should go into public service.

In 1946, following a brief career as a journalist, Kennedy ran for the House of Representatives in the overwhelmingly Democratic Eleventh Congressional District of Massachusetts. After winning a tough primary fight in a Democratic district, he won an easy election victory. He was reelected in 1948 and again in 1950, each time with increasingly larger margins of victory. In Congress he gained a reputation as a moderate, but he consistently supported the social welfare programs he felt were essential to the working people in his district.

In 1952, he decided to run for the Senate against incumbent Henry Cabot Lodge, whom he beat decisively by 70,000 votes. In the Senate, where he served at various times on the Government Operations Committee, the Labor and Public Welfare Committee and the Foreign Relations Committee, he continued to develop his record as a moderate.

In 1953 he married Jacqueline Lee Bouvier, and the Kennedys quickly became one of the most attractive couples in the Washington social life. Later, in 1954, he underwent a critical operation to correct his back injury. While recuperating in the hospital, he wrote a book, *Profiles in Courage*—a collection of short biographies about men in public life who had shown courage in standing up for their principles. It was awarded the 1957 Pulitzer Prize for Biography.

However, it was not until 1956 that Kennedy emerged as a national figure. At the Democratic National Convention, Governor Adlai Stevenson received the presidential nomination and threw the vice-presidential nomination to the convention floor. This was an unprecedented procedure; usually the presidential nominee picks his running mate. Although Senator Estes Kefauver won the vice-presidential nomination, Kennedy showed surprising strength in the balloting. By the time the convention ended television coverage had made Kennedy a popular national figure, and he was soon considered a serious contender for the 1960 Democratic presidential nomination. He was taken even more seriously after he won reelection to the Senate in 1958 by a record-breaking 869,000 votes.

In January of 1959, Kennedy announced his presidential candidacy and, during the spring, he entered and won several important presidential primaries—including those in New Hampshire, Wisconsin, Illinois, and West Virginia. In July, at the Democratic Convention in Los Angeles, he was nominated on the first ballot and chose Senator Lyndon B. Johnson of Texas as his vice-presidential running mate. His opponent was Vice-President Richard Nixon. Each candidate waged a vigorous campaign, the climax coming when Kennedy challenged Nixon to a series of nationwide television debates. Kennedy performed well in these debates, and it is generally conceded that they were a critical factor in the election, which Kennedy won by a narrow margin of 118,574 out of more than 68 million votes cast.

LYNDON B. JOHNSON: EARLY CAREER

Lyndon B. Johnson was born on a ranch near Johnson City, Texas, in 1908. He went to local schools, and, after graduating from high school in 1924, he worked for a few years at different jobs before entering Southwest Texas State Teacher's College in 1927. Although he took a year off to teach school in Cotula, Texas, he graduated in 1930 with a B.S. degree in history and social science. He also was on the debating team, edited the campus newspaper and organized a new campus political group. His first job after college was teaching public speaking at a Houston High School.

But his main interest was politics. In 1931 he helped Richard M. Kleberg to campaign and win a special congressional election. Then he went to

Senate Majority Leader Lyndon Johnson (l.) discusses legislation in 1951 with Senators Wayne Morse of Oregon and Richard Russell of Georgia.

(The Lyndon B. Johnson Library)

work for Kleberg in Washington. Johnson, an avid Democrat, worked for several years on Capitol Hill, where his father's old friend, Sam Rayburn (eventually to become Speaker of the House) became his mentor. In 1934, Johnson married the former Claudia Alta Taylor, better known as Lady Bird.

In 1935, Franklin Roosevelt appointed Johnson administrator of the Texas National Youth Administration. In this job he helped thirty thousand young Texans find work, which made Johnson a well-known figure in his state. Early in 1937, a House of Representatives seat became available and Johnson ran for it against eight other candidates on a platform one hundred per cent in support of Franklin Roosevelt and the New Deal. He won, launching a career in the House which lasted until 1946.

In Washington, President Roosevelt took a liking to Johnson and helped advance his career, although Roosevelt's support did not help Johnson win a Texas Senate seat in a special election held in 1941. During World War II, Johnson served in the Navy as special representative for the president in Australia and New Zealand. He received the Silver Star for gallantry in action when a bomber in which he was flying was damaged by bullets. After the war, he returned to the House, where he served on the House Committee on postwar policy, the Armed Services Committee and the Joint Atomic Energy Committee.

In 1948, Johnson entered the Democratic primary to run for the Senate. He placed second to former Governor Coke Johnson, then defeated him in a run-off by eighty-seven votes, and this won Johnson the nickname, "Landslide Lyndon." He beat his Republican opponent in the main election and was reelected to the Senate in 1954. Johnson quickly became a powerful leader in the Senate. In 1951 and 1952, as the Democratic Majority Whip, his main task was to get Democratic senators to the floor of the Senate to vote. In 1953, he was elected Minority Leader (the Republicans had won control of the Congress in 1952) and after the Democrats regained control of the Congress in 1954, he was elected Majority Leader. In this post, he was regarded as one of the most effective legislative leaders in the Senate's history. During Eisenhower's administration, Johnson was also acclaimed for his

role as leader of the opposition, especially in the conduct of U.S. foreign policy.

By 1960, Johnson was probably the most powerful man in his party and a serious candidate for the presidential nomination. However, he lost to John F. Kennedy, who nevertheless recognized Johnson's stature and influence by asking him to run as his vice-president. It is generally believed that Johnson's campaigning in the South helped Kennedy win his narrow victory in 1960.

Johnson was an energetic and hard-working vice-president, especially in his effort to push Kennedy's legislative program through Congress. Kennedy kept him well-briefed as vice-president—which was fortunate because, in 1963, Lyndon Johnson abruptly became president of the United States, when John F. Kennedy was assassinated.

The road to the White House usually begins when powerful members of a political party consider a candidate popular enough to win votes in all parts of the country. Between 1928 and 1932, Democrats began to talk about Franklin D. Roosevelt, the governor of New York, as a good presidential candidate. Alfred E. Smith (standing) who had been the Democratic presidential candidate in 1928, shakes hands with Governor Roosevelt (left) in the Governor's office in Albany. The photograph was taken in 1930. (The Franklin D. Roosevelt Library)

In recent years, with numerous senators running for president, the fashionable place to make the announcement of their candidacy has been in the historic Senate Caucus Room in the Old Senate Office Building. But in 1952, General Dwight D. Eisenhower (above) returned to his home town of Abilene to announce his candidacy on a rainy night in June. *(Gifford Hampshire)*

During the primaries, campaign workers in every state are working to round up delegates who will promise to vote for their candidate at the convention. This complicated political process often involves making promises to powerful political leaders. It is also a critical part of seeking election to the presidency, because a serious contender must become the candidate of one of the two major political parties. A person can run for the presidency on a third-party ticket, but no "third party" candidate has been elected president in American history. Of course, an incumbent president, eligible for another term, as Lyndon Johnson was in 1964, is virtually assured of the presidential nomination. After the nomination is in hand, the next step is to select a running mate—the vice-presidential candidate. He is usually picked to add strength to the ticket in a certain area of the country or with certain groups of voters. (Below) President Johnson accepting the nomination at the 1964 Democratic Convention in Atlantic City. To his left is his vice-presidential choice, Senator Hubert Humphrey. *(The Lyndon B. Johnson Library)*

A candidate, especially one who is not the clear choice of his party leaders, usually declares his candidacy in January. This enables him to enter the party's presidential primaries to test his vote-getting strength. The objective is to try to win in several state primaries so as to go into the party convention not only having demonstrated popularity but with a number of delegates to the convention pledged to vote for him. (Above) Senator Kennedy campaigns in the 1960 California primary. *(The Democratic Digest)*

After the convention, held late in the summer, the candidates take time off for a rest and to organize their campaign, which usually begins on Labor Day and runs until the second Tuesday in November. Once the campaign is underway, the candidates' primary objective is to get their "message" across to the people. The presidential candidates use the radio, personal appearances, television, commercials, newspaper advertisements—any way they think will effectively get their position on the issues known to the voters. (*The Herbert Hoover Library*)

Franklin Roosevelt in the 1932 campaign. (*The Franklin D. Roosevelt Library*)

Harry Truman speaks from his favorite platform. (*U.S. Navy*)

The nature of a presidential campaign is determined by the issues and by the candidates' proposed solutions to the problems facing the nation. In a time of peace and prosperity, the candidates usually promise more of the same or better. In time of crisis, the candidates promise to try to bring the nation out of its troubles. In 1932, for example, Franklin Roosevelt (shown campaigning, above) promised to end the Depression. And in 1952, General Eisenhower promised to "go to Korea" in an effort to help end the Korean war. In December 1952, after his election but before his inauguration, Ike did go to Korea (below) and he did end the war in Korea.

Lyndon Johnson goes out to meet the people in the 1964 presidential campaign. (The Lyndon B. Johnson Library)

Although not a candidate in 1960, President Eisenhower draws a lot of attention when he casts his ballot at the firehouse in Gettysburg. *(The Dwight D. Eisenhower Library)*

When the campaign finally comes to an end early in November, the candidates usually go home—to vote and anxiously await the outcome of the election. As the returns come in, there is unrestrained joy in the victor's camp—and then a triumphant journey to Washington, especially for an incumbent president who has been returned to office.

Herbert Hoover and his family return to their home in Palo Alto to await the outcome of the 1932 election. *(The Herbert Hoover Library)*

ELECTION NIGHT

President Eisenhower in 1956 shows what it feels like to be the winner. *(The Dwight D. Eisenhower Library)*

And, in this famous photograph, President Truman shows what it feels like to be a "loser." Actually, Truman beat Dewey in 1948 in one of the greatest upsets in political history. *(United Press International)*

Election Day to the inauguration is a two-and-a-half-month period of well-deserved rest for the president-elect and his staff. During this time, the new president usually begins to form his administration and prepares his inaugural address, which will set forth his objectives for the next four years. After the president takes the oath of office, on January 20 following the election year, he delivers his inaugural address on the steps of the Capitol. Then he rides to the White House, where he and his family preside over several days of inaugural ceremonies. (right) President Truman is sworn in by Chief Justice Fred Vinson in 1949. *(Harris-Ewing/The Harry S. Truman Library)*

Herbert Hoover delivered his inaugural address in 1929. He opened the main body of the address by saying: "If we survey the situation of our Nation both at home and abroad, we find many satisfactions, we find some causes for concern. . . ."

But as most presidents do in their inaugural address, he concluded on a note of hope and promise: "Ours is a land rich in resources; stimulating in its glorious beauty; filled with millions of happy homes; blessed with comfort and opportunity. In no nation are the institutions of progress more advanced. In no nation are the fruits of accomplishment more secure. In no nation is the government more worthy of respect. . . ." *(The Herbert Hoover Library)*

4

THE PRESIDENT, CONGRESS AND THE LAWS OF THE LAND

The only relations between the Congress and the president specified in the Constitution, are that the president must periodically report on the state of the union, recommend legislation, convene the Congress, and adjourn it if the Congress cannot agree on its own adjournment. And, of course, he approves or disapproves and enforces all laws passed by Congress—although Congress can override a presidential veto with a vote of two-thirds of both houses. Historically, however, the president's role in the recommendation and passage of our nation's laws has proven much greater than the framers of the Constitution anticipated. (*Below*) President Roosevelt signs a congressional bill into a law of the land.

(The Franklin D. Roosevelt Library)

(Below) President Truman delivers the 1950 state of the union message to a joint session of Congress. In his annual message, the president outlines, in broad terms, the legislative program he plans to submit to Congress for that session. Later, when he sends up a major bill, he usually submits a "special message" concerning that bill. *(The Harry S. Truman Library)*

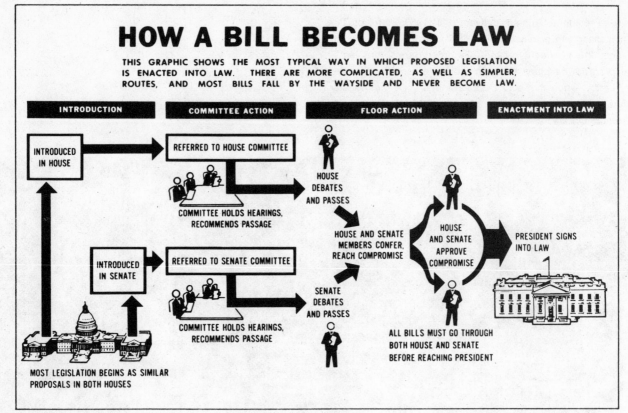

HOW A BILL BECOMES LAW

THIS GRAPHIC SHOWS THE MOST TYPICAL WAY IN WHICH PROPOSED LEGISLATION IS ENACTED INTO LAW. THERE ARE MORE COMPLICATED, AS WELL AS SIMPLER, ROUTES, AND MOST BILLS FALL BY THE WAYSIDE AND NEVER BECOME LAW.

INTRODUCTION

INTRODUCED IN HOUSE

INTRODUCED IN SENATE

MOST LEGISLATION BEGINS AS SIMILAR PROPOSALS IN BOTH HOUSES

COMMITTEE ACTION

REFERRED TO HOUSE COMMITTEE

COMMITTEE HOLDS HEARINGS, RECOMMENDS PASSAGE

REFERRED TO SENATE COMMITTEE

COMMITTEE HOLDS HEARINGS, RECOMMENDS PASSAGE

FLOOR ACTION

HOUSE DEBATES AND PASSES

SENATE DEBATES AND PASSES

HOUSE AND SENATE MEMBERS CONFER, REACH COMPROMISE

HOUSE AND SENATE APPROVE COMPROMISE

ALL BILLS MUST GO THROUGH BOTH HOUSE AND SENATE BEFORE REACHING PRESIDENT

ENACTMENT INTO LAW

PRESIDENT SIGNS INTO LAW

Reprinted from Congressional Quarterly

As the above chart shows, all bills must originate in the Congress, which means that the president's bills must actually be submitted by a senator or congressman—usually a member of his own party. This calls for many legislative strategy sessions between the president and the congressional leaders to determine who will handle which bills and how they will be supported in Congress. (Below) President Kennedy and his vice-president, Lyndon Johnson (center), discuss Kennedy's legislative program with the Senate Majority Leader, Hubert Humphrey. *(The John F. Kennedy Library)*

Most bills proposed in Congress—even the president's—never pass, and it can take years before they become law. If the president wants results, he must spend a lot of time developing good congressional relations. (Below) President Johnson attends one of his regular breakfasts with congressional leaders of both parties. His grandson, Patrick Lyndon Nugent, temporarily joined this particular meeting. *(The Lyndon B. Johnson Library)*

A president expects his Cabinet and other members of the administration to help in the enactment of his legislative program. (Right) In 1930, President Hoover (second from left) and his whole Cabinet visited Congress as the adjournment hour approached. *(The Herbert Hoover Library)*

The president tries to keep the people informed about his legislative program, hoping that they will write their congressmen in support of his bills. (Left) President Eisenhower discusses one of his legislative proposals at a 1957 press conference. *(The Dwight D. Eisenhower Library)*

Another way for a president to enlist support for his legislation is through the state political leaders. (Below) In 1939, President Roosevelt entertains a group of twenty-three state governors for lunch at his home in Hyde Park. *(The Franklin D. Roosevelt Library)*

Mostly, though, it comes down to the president's ability, one way or another, to persuade Congress that his proposed legislation is essential. Here President Johnson, one of the most persuasive legislative strategists in the nation's history, discusses one of his bills with congressional leader, Representative Carl Albert. *(The Lyndon B. Johnson Library)*

When a major bill is finally passed by Congress, there is a bill-signing ceremony, usually in the White House, and congressional leaders are invited to attend. The president usually makes a short speech, and the pens used to sign the bill are given to the congressmen who sponsored the bill or worked hard to get it passed. (Above) President Hoover signs the Farm Relief Bill in 1929. (Right) A number of pens are used by President Johnson in the signing of a bill.

(The Lyndon B. Johnson Library)

Once a bill becomes law, it is the president's job to enforce it, either by bringing public pressure to bear on the violators or working through the law-enforcement agencies and the Department of Justice and, if necessary, he is empowered to use federal troops. (Left) President Eisenhower explains to the nation his decision to use federal troops, in 1957, to force Governor Faubus of Arkansas to comply with the school desegregation laws. *(The Dwight D. Eisenhower Library)*

The president's principal allies in the enforcement of laws are the Department of Justice and the Federal Bureau of Investigation. (Below) President Kennedy talks with his brother, Robert Kennedy, whom he had just appointed Attorney General, and FBI Director, J. Edgar Hoover. *(The John F. Kennedy Library)*

Final decision as to whether a law violates the Constitution rests with the courts, especially the Supreme Court of the United States. Under our system of government, with its checks and balances, the Congress and the president pass the laws, but the Supreme Court may be called upon to decide whether a given law is in violation of the Constitu-tion. Supreme Court justices are appointed by the president, with the advice and consent of the Senate. (Above) President Truman and Chief Justice Fred Vinson lay the corner-stone of the U.S. Courts Building in Washington. (Below) President Johnson meets with Chief Justice Earl Warren after taking office in 1963.

5

THE PRESIDENT'S JOBS—I:

Chief Executive

The president is, first of all, the chief executive of the United States and administrator of the constantly expanding federal bureaucracy. He is also the architect of American foreign policy and commander in chief of the armed forces. Finally, he is the ceremonial leader of all the American people and leader of his political party. He is also a human being who needs rest, recreation and time to spend with his family.

The burdens of the presidency have always been a topic of concern. "Forty years ago, in 1899," President Franklin D. Roosevelt said, "President

McKinley could deal with the whole machinery of government through his eight cabinet secretaries and heads of two commissions . . . and he could keep in touch with all the work through eight or ten persons. Now, forty years later, not only do some thirty major agencies (to say nothing of the minor ones) report directly to the President, there are several quasi-judicial bodies which have enough administrative work to require them also to see him on important executive matters. It has become physically impossible for one man to see so many persons, to receive reports directly from them, and to attempt to advise them on their problems which they submit. . . ." That statement was made in 1939, before the outbreak of World War II. Inevitably, as the country continues to grow and the people turn to the government for more and more services, the government continues to expand. And so do the president's responsibilities.

President Eisenhower and his Cabinet members pose for a photograph preceding a meeting in 1953. (Left to right, seated) Henry Cabot Lodge, Douglas McKay, George Humphrey, Richard Nixon, Herbert Brownell, Sinclair Weeks, Oveta Culp Hobby, Sherman Adams, Joseph Dodge, Arthur Flemming, Martin Durkin, Arthur Summerfield, John Foster Dulles, President Eisenhower, Charles Wilson, Ezra Benson, Harold Stassen. (Standing) Philip Young, Robert Cutler. *(The Dwight D. Eisenhower Library)*

EXECUTIVE OFFICE OF THE PRESIDENT

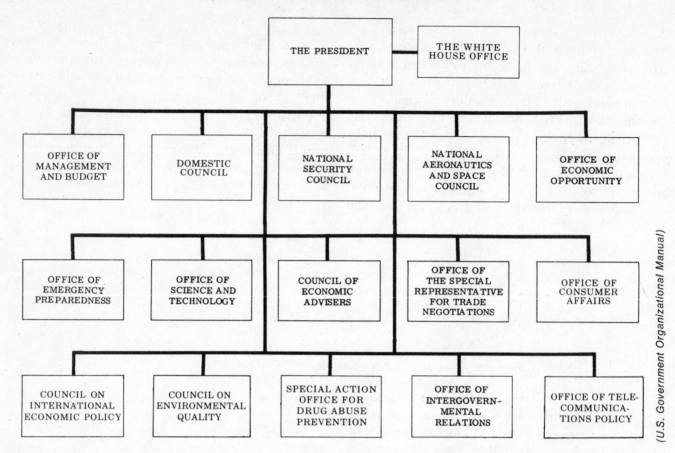

THE PRESIDENT

THE WHITE HOUSE OFFICE

OFFICE OF MANAGEMENT AND BUDGET

DOMESTIC COUNCIL

NATIONAL SECURITY COUNCIL

NATIONAL AERONAUTICS AND SPACE COUNCIL

OFFICE OF ECONOMIC OPPORTUNITY

OFFICE OF EMERGENCY PREPAREDNESS

OFFICE OF SCIENCE AND TECHNOLOGY

COUNCIL OF ECONOMIC ADVISERS

OFFICE OF THE SPECIAL REPRESENTATIVE FOR TRADE NEGOTIATIONS

OFFICE OF CONSUMER AFFAIRS

COUNCIL ON INTERNATIONAL ECONOMIC POLICY

COUNCIL ON ENVIRONMENTAL QUALITY

SPECIAL ACTION OFFICE FOR DRUG ABUSE PREVENTION

OFFICE OF INTERGOVERN-MENTAL RELATIONS

OFFICE OF TELE-COMMUNICA-TIONS POLICY

(U.S. Government Organizational Manual)

Today, the executive office of the president is a vast, complex organization. At the center of this administrative organization is the president. And at his side, although without direct responsibility, is the vice-president. Considering that two vice-presidents in recent years have suddenly become presidents, it is essential that the vice-president be briefed at all times about the programs, policies and objectives of the administration. (Below) President Johnson meets with his vice-president, Hubert Humphrey, in the White House Cabinet Room.

(The Lyndon B. Johnson Library)

Every president needs the help of a close personal staff —usually men and women he has known for a long time who have come to know his needs and moods. (Right) President Roosevelt with his secretary, Marguerite LeHand. *(The Franklin D. Roosevelt Library)*

He also needs a close aide who can, on occasion, even speak for him. Kennedy's was Theodore Sorensen, on the left. *(The John F. Kennedy Library)*

As every president knows, the key to good government administration is the selection of competent people. As President Hoover (below) said: "The President himself cannot pretend to know or to have the time for detailed investigation into every one of the hundreds of subjects in a great people. But the fine minds of our citizens are available and can be utilized for the search." *(The Herbert Hoover Library)*

THE GOVERNMENT OF THE UNITED STATES

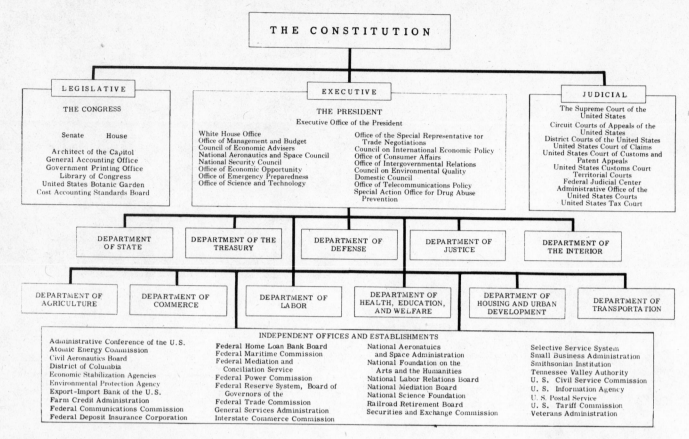

THE CONSTITUTION

LEGISLATIVE

THE CONGRESS

Senate   House

Architect of the Capitol
General Accounting Office
Government Printing Office
Library of Congress
United States Botanic Garden
Cost Accounting Standards Board

EXECUTIVE

THE PRESIDENT
Executive Office of the President

White House Office
Office of Management and Budget
Council of Economic Advisers
National Aeronautics and Space Council
National Security Council
Office of Economic Opportunity
Office of Emergency Preparedness
Office of Science and Technology

Office of the Special Representative for
Trade Negotiations
Council on International Economic Policy
Office of Consumer Affairs
Office of Intergovernmental Relations
Council on Environmental Quality
Domestic Council
Office of Telecommunications Policy
Special Action Office for Drug Abuse
Prevention

JUDICIAL

The Supreme Court of the
United States
Circuit Courts of Appeals of the
United States
District Courts of the United States
United States Court of Claims
United States Court of Customs and
Patent Appeals
United States Customs Court
Territorial Courts
Federal Judicial Center
Administrative Office of the
United States Courts
United States Tax Court

| DEPARTMENT OF STATE | DEPARTMENT OF THE TREASURY | DEPARTMENT OF DEFENSE | DEPARTMENT OF JUSTICE | DEPARTMENT OF THE INTERIOR |

| DEPARTMENT OF AGRICULTURE | DEPARTMENT OF COMMERCE | DEPARTMENT OF LABOR | DEPARTMENT OF HEALTH, EDUCATION, AND WELFARE | DEPARTMENT OF HOUSING AND URBAN DEVELOPMENT | DEPARTMENT OF TRANSPORTATION |

INDEPENDENT OFFICES AND ESTABLISHMENTS

Administrative Conference of the U.S.
Atomic Energy Commission
Civil Aeronautics Board
District of Columbia
Economic Stabilization Agencies
Environmental Protection Agency
Export-Import Bank of the U.S.
Farm Credit Administration
Federal Communications Commission
Federal Deposit Insurance Corporation

Federal Home Loan Bank Board
Federal Maritime Commission
Federal Mediation and
Conciliation Service
Federal Power Commission
Federal Reserve System, Board of
Governors of the
Federal Trade Commission
General Services Administration
Interstate Commerce Commission

National Aeronautics
and Space Administration
National Foundation on the
Arts and the Humanities
National Labor Relations Board
National Mediation Board
National Science Foundation
Railroad Retirement Board
Securities and Exchange Commission

Selective Service System
Small Business Administration
Smithsonian Institution
Tennessee Valley Authority
U. S. Civil Service Commission
U. S. Information Agency
U. S. Postal Service
U. S. Tariff Commission
Veterans Administration

(The U.S. Government Organization Manual)

(The Franklin D. Roosevelt Library)

Beginning with the men to head the eleven executive departments, which make up his Cabinet, the president must find hundreds of men to help him run the huge bureaucracy that the government has become. (Left) Franklin Roosevelt congratulates Frank Knox, in 1940, whom he appointed Secretary of the Navy.

The president can also turn to special assistants appointed to carry out specific assignments in some area of public affairs. Nelson Rockefeller (right) held several such assignments in the Eisenhower administration. "I believe," said President Eisenhower, "that the Presidency should be relieved of detail and many of its activities given to proper officials who can take delegated authority and exercise it in his name." (The Dwight D. Eisenhower Library)

"The President may have an adviser who is not a Cabinet member," said President Truman, "although all Cabinet members are advisers. There are some special issues on which the President needs detailed information from experts, and it is customary to try to discover the man who is best informed on these detailed matters." (Left) President Truman (center) swears in Averell Harriman in 1951 as his Director of Mutual Security. Chief Justice Vinson (right) administers the oath. (The Harry S. Truman Library)

The budget for operating the federal government today runs into billions of dollars. The money must be appropriated by Congress, acting on budget recommendations made, at the beginning of each year, by the president. Often, Congress will not grant the president as much money as he and his advisers request and, sometimes, Congress adds

(Y. R. Okamuto/The Lyndon B. Johnson Library)

money to projects important to either house. (Above) President Johnson and his economic advisers discuss the budget with members of Congress. (Below) President Hoover signs a Rivers and Harbors Bill in 1930, as a group of congressmen look on.

(The Herbert Hoover Library)

A huge army of government employees works for the government agencies. They are appointed by the Civil Service to help run the government. (Above) President Truman speaks at the annual awards ceremony for the Department of Agriculture. (The Harry S. Truman Library)

Despite the help he gets from his Cabinet members, special assistants and government employees, the final responsibility for running the government rests with the president. President Truman (right) used to keep a sign on his desk that said, "The Buck Stops Here." "Under the Constitution," said Truman, "the President of the United States is alone responsible for the 'faithful execution of the laws.' Our government is fixed on the basis that the President is the only person in the Executive Branch who has the final authority. Everyone else in the Executive Branch is an agent of the President." (The Harry S. Truman Library)

Traditionally, the president begins every year with a state of the union address to Congress in which he discusses general conditions of the country and calls on the people to work hard to help achieve his goals. (Above) President Eisenhower delivers his 1954 state of the union message. Seated behind him are Vice-President Richard Nixon and Speaker of the House Joseph Martin. *(The Dwight D. Eisenhower Library)*

When the nation has economic problems, the president must make a special effort to solve them. (Below) President Hoover presides at a 1932 meeting of business and administration leaders seeking to improve economic conditions. *(The Herbert Hoover Library)*

The president tries to keep the people confident in the basic soundness of the economy. If there are problems, he makes every effort to assure them that the problems are only temporary and are being dealt with properly. In 1933, President Roosevelt (right) launched a series of "fireside chats" on the radio to keep people informed on the state of the nation. (Below) President Kennedy reports on the state of the economy via television in 1962.

(The Franklin D. Roosevelt Library)

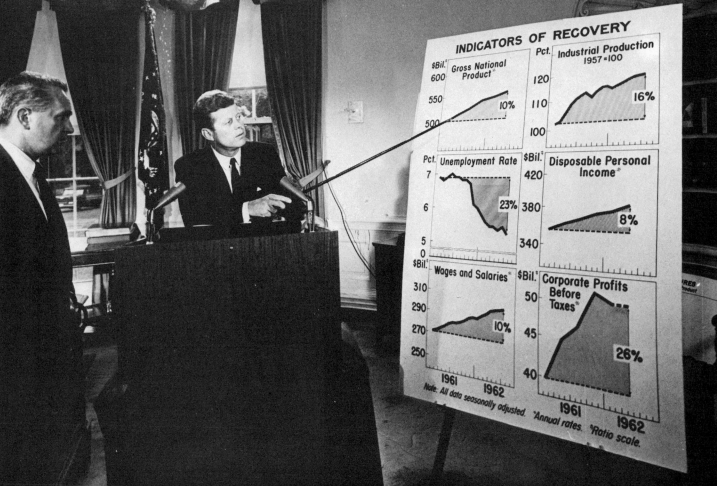

(The John F. Kennedy Library)

The president tries to get around the country to see for himself what conditions are like, and he tries to keep in touch with farmers and workers. (Above) President Eisenhower visits a farm in Oklahoma. To his left is his secretary of agriculture, Ezra Taft Benson. (The Dwight D. Eisenhower Library)

President Roosevelt in Jamestown, North Dakota, 1936. (The Franklin D. Roosevelt Library)

President Johnson visits a job training center in Philadelphia.
(The Lyndon B. Johnson Library)

A group of American Federation of Labor workers greets
President Truman in Kansas City. (The Kansas City Star)

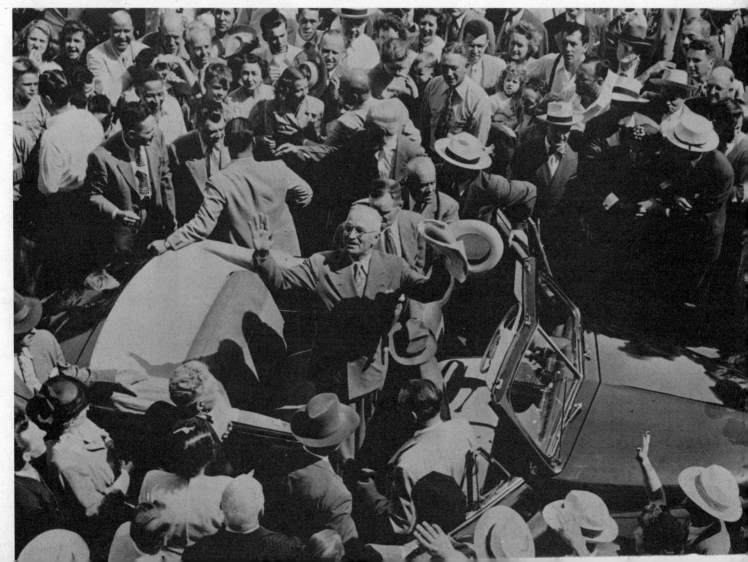

President Truman with members of an industry advisory council. *(The Harry S. Truman Library)*

Labor leaders meet in the White House with President Johnson. *(The Lyndon B. Johnson Library)*

President Johnson presides at a meeting of his Labor Management Advisory Committee. *(The Lyndon B. Johnson Library)*

Settlement of an airlines strike is announced by President Kennedy and his secretary of labor, Arthur Goldberg. *(The John F. Kennedy Library)*

For a healthy economy, it is essential that labor and management get along, and the president makes every effort to keep the two groups working together. When there is a dispute between labor and management, especially in an industry vital to the public, the president will try to enforce arbitration and bring about a speedy settlement.

In recent years, social services and civil rights have taken more and more of the president's time. (Above) President Hoover meets with representatives of welfare organizations on the White House lawn in 1929. (Below) President Eisenhower poses for a photograph before discussing civil rights problems with a group of black leaders in 1958.

President Kennedy addresses a senior citizens conference in 1963. *(The John F. Kennedy Library)*

The emphasis on social services has made the Department of Health, Education and Welfare one of the largest and most critical government agencies, commanding much of the president's time. (Below) President Johnson talks to employees and officials of the National Institutes of Health, an agency of HEW. *(National Institutes of Health)*

White House Press Secretary James Hagerty briefs President Eisenhower. *(The Dwight D. Eisenhower Library)*

One of the president's primary concerns is the media—newspapers, radio, television and magazines. "The President's relations with the press," said President Truman, "are of the utmost importance. By way of the press he maintains a direct contact with the people."

The president's relations with the press are handled through the White House press secretary, who schedules all interviews and press conferences. The secretary also meets with the press daily to answer questions about the president's position on various issues. This means that the president is constantly working with his press secretary—being briefed by him on what the press wants to know or telling him his own views to be passed on to the press. The questions from the press are usually well-informed, which means that the president must himself keep thoroughly informed about everything that is going on in the country and what the press is saying about his administration. He does this through daily press summaries prepared by the White House staff and by reading as much as he can.

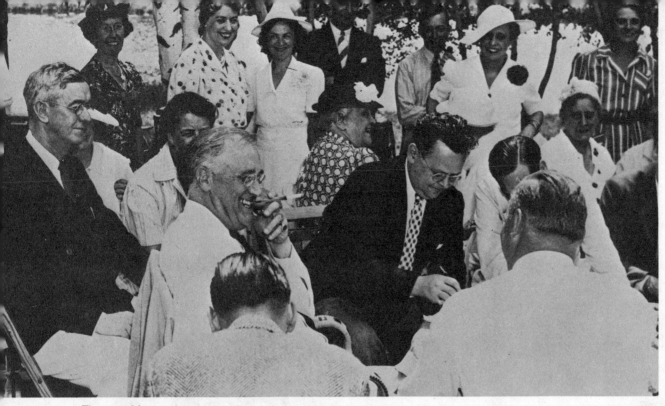

The president, of course, often meets with the press or consents to interviews. (Above) President Roosevelt holds an informal press conference at his home in Hyde Park. (*The Franklin D. Roosevelt Library*)

President Kennedy holds a press conference. Seated to his left are Press Secretary Pierre Salinger and his assistant, Andrew Hatcher. (*The John F. Kennedy Library*)

President Roosevelt being photographed for a newsreel in 1932. *(The Franklin D. Roosevelt Library)*

The president devotes as much time as possible to meeting with the press on formal and informal occasions. (Right) President Hoover addresses an annual meeting of the Associated Press. (Below) President Kennedy entertains a group of California editors and publishers at a White House luncheon. (Facing page, above) President Truman with the winners of a White House photographers' contest. (Facing page, below) President Kennedy at a meeting of the American Editorial Cartoonists Association.

(The Herbert Hoover Library)

(The John F. Kennedy Library)

Despite his efforts to keep on friendly terms with reporters, the president cannot avoid criticism in the press. Editorial writers, columnists, and especially the cartoonists do not restrain themselves in attacking the president when they think he is wrong. They can also (right) show some sympathy for the president. *(J. N. Ding/The Herbert Hoover Library)*

The U. S. award for distinguished service.

However, the president must ignore his critics and do what he thinks is right—especially in a time of crisis when his primary duty, as chief executive, is to provide leadership. (Left) President Hoover, in 1931, speaks to American Legionnaires in Detroit, urging them to discontinue their demands for additional veterans' bonus payments. *(The Herbert Hoover Library)*

President Roosevelt visits a Civilian Conservation Corps camp during the Depression. *(The Franklin D. Roosevelt Library)*

President Kennedy prepares to address the nation, in 1962, during the crisis that arose when the University of Mississippi refused to admit the black student James Meredith. *(The John F. Kennedy Library)*

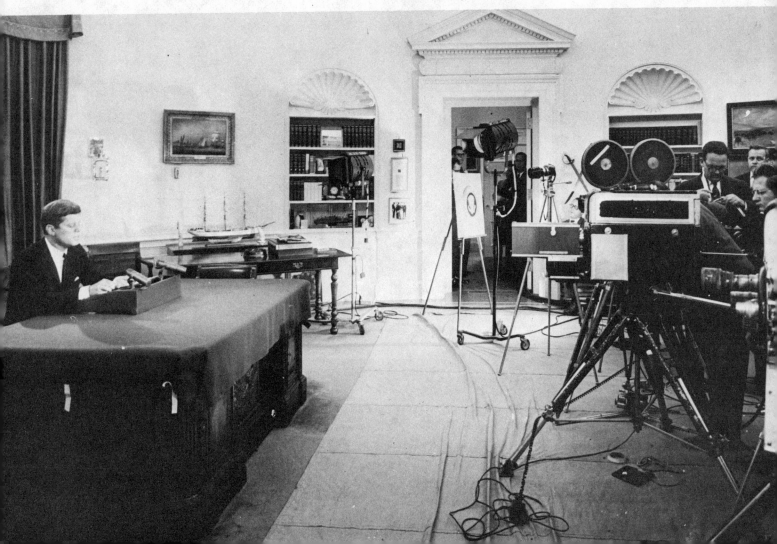

"The President," said Dwight Eisenhower, "has to be concerned with everything that happens to any human being in the United States and often abroad. . . . One of the things about the Presidency is the way you have to be prepared to jump just like a mountain sheep from one jag to another jag and you're always on the alert." (Below) President Eisenhower surveys a midwestern drought area in 1957. With him are Secretary of the Interior Fred Seaton (standing) and Secretary of Agriculture Ezra Taft Benson. *(The Dwight D. Eisenhower Library)*

Perhaps the best summary of the president's role as chief executive was provided by Harry S. Truman. "As President of the United States," he said, "I am guided by a simple formula: to do, in all cases . . . what seems to me to be best for the welfare of the people." (Opposite page) President Truman prepares to deliver a Fourth of July address at the Washington Monument. *(The Harry S. Truman Library)*

6

THE PRESIDENT'S JOBS—II:

**Architect of Foreign Policy; Commander in Chief
of the Armed Forces**

The president "shall have the power, by and with the Advice and Consent of the Senate, to make Treaties . . . and he shall nominate, and, by and with the Advice and Consent of the Senate, he shall appoint Ambassadors, other public Ministers and Consuls . . . he shall receive Ambassadors and other public ministers. . . ."

Tnat is all the Constitution says about the presi-dent and his authority to conduct foreign affairs. But there is little doubt today about who has this responsibility. There is, in fact, no other elected official or branch of government in a position to conduct U.S. relations with other nations. From George Washington's time to the present, the final responsibility and authority in almost every aspect of foreign affairs has rested with the president.

President Roosevelt studies a globe of the world presented to him by the U.S. Army on Christmas, 1942. *(The Franklin D. Roosevelt Library)*

The president's principal foreign affairs advisor is his secretary of state. "It is immensely important," said President Truman, "that these two men . . . understand each other completely and that they know what their respective roles are. The Secretary of State should never at any time come to think that he is the man in the White House, and the President should not try to be the Secretary of State." However, the trend in more recent years has been for the president to act more and more as his own secretary of state. (Above) President Truman looks on as Chief Justice Fred Vinson (right) swears in General George C. Marshall as secretary of state in 1947. *(The Harry S. Truman Library)*

The president also calls on numerous other officials and assistants—Cabinet members, White House aides and directors of special government agencies, such as the U.S. Information Agency—to help him formulate U.S. foreign policy. (Below) President Johnson meets with his top foreign affairs advisors at a White House luncheon in January 1968. *(The Lyndon B. Johnson Library)*

The president appoints all ambassadors, and before they go to their posts he usually discusses with them special problems of the country to which they are assigned. Often he will send a personal message to be delivered to the head of that country. (Below) President Kennedy talks with William Attwood, the newly appointed ambassador to the West African country of Guinea. The president was angry because President Sekou Toure of Guinea had suggested that Kennedy might have had something to do with the assassination of the African leader Patrice Lumumba. He told Attwood to remind Toure that the assassination had occurred before Kennedy had been sworn in as president. (*Paul Fusco*/Look *magazine*)

The Senate must approve of ambassadorial appointments and treaties and the House of Representatives must appropriate the money needed for the conduct of our foreign affairs. It is, therefore, essential that the president work closely with the Congress in this area. (Left) President Johnson discusses foreign policy with Senator William Fulbright, Chairman of the Senate Foreign Relations Committee. *(The Lyndon B. Johnson Library)*

(The Franklin D. Roosevelt Library)

(The Herbert Hoover Library)

The president meets continually with foreign ambassadors, prime ministers and other ranking foreign officials and dignitaries who come to the United States. (Above) Russian Ambassador Vyacheslav Molotov confers with President Franklin D. Roosevelt in 1942; (right) President Hoover (left) and his secretary of state, Henry L. Stimson (right), pose with Italian Foreign Minister Dino Grandi after a 1931 conference.

The president negotiates and signs all treaties between the United States and foreign powers. (Above) President Hoover signs a 1930 naval treaty in London. *(The Herbert Hoover Library)*

Every president is responsible for the development of America's dependent territories overseas. Here, President Roosevelt, in 1935, approves the new Constitution of the Philippines, which later was granted complete independence. *(The Franklin D. Roosevelt Library)*

A primary concern of the president is international trade and currency. (Above) President Hoover, in 1930, prepares to inaugurate radio-telephone service between the United States and Latin America, which was an important step in improving commerce in the Western Hemisphere. (Below) President Johnson, his economic advisors, and key members of Congress meet in 1967 to discuss the effect of the British devaluation of the pound on the U.S. dollar.

When a head of a foreign state arrives for a formal visit, it is an occasion for high ceremony. (Above) President Roosevelt greets the king of England (left) at Washington's Union Station in 1939. At the right is the queen; to her right is Mrs. Roosevelt. (Below) President Kennedy takes India's Prime Minister Nehru on a review of the troops in 1961; (facing page) Kennedy escorts President Radhakaishan of India to the White House in 1963.

WELCOME PRESIDENT RADHAKRISHNAN OF INDIA

(The White House)

At some point during the ceremonies, there are serious discussions about matters of concern to the president and the foreign leader. The visits frequently end with a formal state dinner accompanied by several speeches and toasts expressing goodwill between the two nations. (Above) President Eisenhower and French President Charles de Gaulle meet in the White House office during de Gaulle's 1960 visit to the United States. (Below) President Truman entertains the Shah of Iran at a state dinner in 1949. "Personal diplomacy" can also take other forms—as when President Johnson (facing page) entertained the Latin American ambassadors to the United States at the LBJ ranch in Texas.

(The Lyndon B. Johnson Library)

(The White House)

The president also has to travel abroad frequently. (Above) President Kennedy boards *Air Force One* to meet with Russian premier Nikita Khrushchev in Vienna and French president Charles de Gaulle in Paris.

When abroad, the president of the United States is always escorted by the head of government, and every foreign country visited by the president of the United States arranges festivities, meetings and ceremonies, which usually end with a reception and a state dinner. (Below) King Paul of Greece rides with President Eisenhower in Athens during his visit to Greece. (Opposite) On their 1966 visit to Seoul, President Johnson and Mrs. Johnson (far left) pose for a photograph before dinner with the president of Korea, H. E. Chung Hee Park and Mrs. Park.

(The Dwight D. Eisenhower Library)

(The Lyndon B. Johnson Library)

When the president returns from a trip abroad, he usually discusses the results of his trip with his aides. President Truman confers with U.S. High Commissioner for Germany, John J. McCloy, and Secretary of State Dean Acheson (right).

(The Harry S. Truman Library)

(The Harry S. Truman Library)

The ultimate goal of every president's foreign policy is the preservation of peace. But since the beginning of the century, this has not been an easy task. There have been two world wars, many tragic, regional wars and, in recent years, a continuing "cold war" with the communist nations, carrying with it the continuing threat of a nuclear war with Russia. Consequently, the president has had to combine his search for peace with constant vigilance and attention to America's natural allies. (Above) President Truman, in 1946, accompanies Winston Churchill to Fulton, Missouri, where the British prime minister gave his famous speech saying that an "iron curtain" had descended over Europe. (Below) President Eisenhower and Secretary of State John Foster Dulles (left) meet with Churchill and British foreign minister Anthony Eden at the White House in 1957.

(The Dwight D. Eisenhower Library)

The president must maintain relations with the Communist nations, despite provocations and incidents that threaten the peace. "Peace does not come by merely wanting it or shouting for it or marching down Main Street for it," said President Johnson. "Peace is built brick by brick. . . ." (Right) President Eisenhower entertains Nikita Khrushchev during the Russian premier's 1959 goodwill tour to the United States. (Below) Soviet Ambassador Anatoly Dobrynin (left) informs President Johnson of the Russian invasion of Czechoslovakia in 1968. With the president is his foreign policy adviser, W. W. Rostow.

(The Dwight D. Eisenhower Library)

(The Lyndon B. Johnson Library)

In search of peace, the president directs U.S. participation in numerous international organizations—including the United Nations. (Right) At the United Nations in 1953, President Eisenhower proposes that all nations concentrate on the peaceful use of atomic energy. (Below) President Kennedy speaks to six hundred Peace Corps volunteers preparing to go abroad in 1962. In his last state of the union address, Kennedy said that "nothing carries the spirit of American idealism and expresses our hopes better and more effectively to the far corners of the earth than does the Peace Corps."

(The Peace Corps)

"Never has there been a President," said Herbert Hoover in a 1929 radio address, "who did not pray that his Administration might be one of peace and that peace should be more assured for his successor. Yet these men have never hesitated when war became the duty of the nation. And always in these years the thought of our Presidents has been adequate preparedness for defense as one of the assurances of peace." (Below) President Hoover makes a plea for peace in a 1930 Memorial Day speech at the Gettysburg battlefield in Pennsylvania. *(The Herbert Hoover Library)*

THE COMMANDER IN CHIEF
IN PEACE AND WAR

The Constitution says specifically that "The President shall be Commander in Chief of the Army and Navy of the United States, and of the Militia of the several States when called into actual service of the United States." This is only logical, for if the president has the responsibility of protecting the national interest in dealing with foreign nations and in defending the country from attack, he must also have the authority to build and maintain a strong system of national defense. Only Congress can declare war. Every one of the six presidents we are observing dealt with some aspects of war, in one way or another: Herbert Hoover helped organize relief for the victims of war in Europe in World War I; Franklin Roosevelt was president during most of World War II; Harry Truman fought in Europe in World War I, and was president when World War II came to an end and during the police action in Korea; Dwight Eisenhower was a professional soldier who commanded American troops in Europe during World War II, and, as president, helped bring the Korean war to an end; John F. Kennedy fought in the Pacific in World War II and was president in the early stages of the Vietnam war; and Lyndon Johnson was a naval officer during World War II and president during the war in Vietnam. However, of the six presidents, only President Roosevelt signed a formal declaration of war, which can only be issued by Congress.

American military might today ranges from small naval patrol boats to incredibly complicated guided missiles capable—with the push of a button—of carrying nuclear warheads to the heart of enemy country. It is a burden of power that no man can take lightly. (Below) President Hoover inspects the crew of the U.S.S. *Salt Lake City* in 1930. (Facing page) President Eisenhower tours the George C. Marshall Space Flight Center in Huntsville, Alabama. With him is Wernher von Braun, one of the scientists who helped develop the guided missile.

(The Herbert Hoover Library)

THE TEAM BEHIND THE SATURN

(The John F. Kennedy Library)

The official on whom the president depends the most for the maintenance of our national defense is the secretary of defense. This is consistent with the American doctrine that military forces should be under civilian control. However, civilian and military leaders are brought together in the Joint Chiefs of Staff and the National Security Council —two executive groups that meet regularly under presidential supervision. (Left) President Kennedy discusses military strategy with his secretary of defense, Robert McNamara, during the Cuban missile crisis. (Below) President Johnson and the Joint Chiefs of Staff meet in the White House.

(The Lyndon B. Johnson Library)

During peacetime, the commander in chief's functions are mostly ceremonial and administrative. (Left) President Hoover decorates Commander Claude Jones with the Congressional Medal of Honor, in 1932, for heroism when the boilers on the U.S.S. *Memphis* exploded. *(The Herbert Hoover Library)*

(Right) A new seal for the Marine Corps is made official by President Eisenhower. *(The Dwight D. Eisenhower Library)*

President Truman at the ceremonies for laying the keel of the atomic submarine, U.S.S. *Nautilus.* *(The Harry S. Truman Library)*

The president is responsible for the nation's space program —which has military implications today because of the importance of rocketry in modern warfare. (Left) Astronaut John Glenn is awarded the Distinguished Service Medal by President Kennedy. *(NASA)*

The weapons of war are costly to a nation and, once they exist, there is always the temptation to use them. For this reason the president, in time of peace, is always anxious to control the buildup of weapons, but only if other nations agree to limit their military forces. (Below) Secretary of War Henry L. Stimson hands President Hoover the official copy of the naval disarmament treaty the president negotiated in London in 1930. *(The Herbert Hoover Library)*

However, the president can never forget that preparedness comes first. (Above) The first name in the national draft system, which is no longer in effect, is drawn by President Roosevelt on October 29, 1940. *(The Franklin D. Roosevelt Library)*

(Below) President Truman attends an Armed Forces Day parade in May 1950 (second from right is General Dwight D. Eisenhower). The strength of the armed forces was critical at that time because the following month the North Koreans invaded South Korea, and the United States, acting under the Charter of the United Nations, went to the defense of the South Koreans. *(Abbie Rowe/The Harry S. Truman Library)*

(The John F. Kennedy Library)

(The Dwight D. Eisenhower Library)

(The Lyndon B. Johnson Library)

96

No president wants war, but he must always be ready to risk the use of force in order to defend the national interest and meet our commitments abroad. (Far left) President Kennedy signs a proclamation in 1961 banning the placement of offensive missiles by any nation on the island of Cuba. (Left) The situation in Berlin, which the Russians were attempting to dominate in violation of the treaties ending World War II, is explained on nationwide television by President Eisenhower. (Facing page, below) In the White House situation room, which is equipped with a communications network for dealing with a military alert, President Johnson tells Secretary of Defense McNamara (on phone) to order the Sixth Fleet to move closer to Syria during the Israeli–Arab war of 1967. The maneuver helped convince the Russians that the United States was ready to intervene if they did. (Below) President Franklin D. Roosevelt declares an unlimited national emergency in May 1941, seven months before Pearl Harbor was attacked.

(The Franklin D. Roosevelt Library)

President Roosevelt signs the declaration of war against Japan on December 8, 1941. A few days later, the Congress also declared war against Germany and Italy. *(The Franklin D. Roosevelt Library)*

(The Franklin D. Roosevelt Library)

When the nation goes to war the president must provide leadership and inspiration for civilians as well as the men in the armed forces. He also assumes responsibility for the general strategy in the war. (Right) President Roosevelt with American troops in Sicily during World War II; with him is General Eisenhower. (Below) President Johnson (with elbow on table) meets with military advisers at the LBJ Ranch in Texas to discuss the situation in Vietnam. To Johnson's left is Secretary of Defense Robert McNamara.

(The Lyndon B. Johnson Library)

As the conflict continues, the president occasionally pays surprise visits to the war zone to help maintain morale and commend his fighting men. (Above) President Johnson presents awards, in 1967, to American troops to Camh Ranh Bay, South Vietnam. *(The Lyndon B. Johnson Library)*

The president has to delegate command to his generals, without relinquishing his superior authority as commander in chief. During the Korean war, the U.S. Far Eastern Commander, General Douglas MacArthur, made several statements regarding U.S. military policy that Truman felt strongly were the prerogative only of the commander in chief. "I could no longer tolerate his insubordination," President Truman said, and removed General MacArthur from his command. (Left) The president with General MacArthur at Wake Island in October 1950, five months before he was forced to fire him. *(U.S. Army/The Harry S. Truman Library)*

In time of war, the president makes every effort to enlist the support of other nations and to work closely with his military allies. And, traditionally, the president tries to ally all the nations of North and South America during a period of crisis. (Above) President Truman addresses a meeting of the Foreign Ministers of the American Republics in March, 1951. (Below) President Roosevelt meets with his wartime ally, British Prime Minister Winston Churchill, at Casablanca, in 1943.

(The Franklin D. Roosevelt Library)

A long and, especially, an unpopular war can exact a heavy toll from a president. The burdens of domestic national affairs, combined with the pressures of fighting a war can wear him down considerably. (Above) A tired President Roosevelt meets with his generals in 1943 at Rabat, Morocco. To his right is General Mark Clark; at the far left is General George Patton. With his back to the camera is presidential aide Harry Hopkins. Two years later, with the war still raging, Roosevelt died of a stroke at Warm Springs, Georgia. (Below) A weary and discouraged President Johnson, in a nationwide television address on March 31, 1968, announces his decision not to be a candidate for reelection so that he can devote all his energies to ending the Vietnam war.

(The Lyndon B. Johnson Library)

When a war finally ends, the president cannot hide his relief when he brings the news to the American people. But although the war may be over, his problems are not. Ahead is the task of leading the country in the postwar world. (Right) President Eisenhower announces the Korean truce to the American people on July 26, 1953. (Below) In 1945, near the end of World War II, Truman poses with British prime minister Winston Churchill and Russian premier Joseph Stalin at the Potsdam Conference, where it became obvious that the East and West had serious differences that would not be resolved for decades.

(The Dwight D. Eisenhower Library)

(The Harry S. Truman Library)

The commander in chief, perhaps more than any man in the country, is aware of the tragedy and destruction of war. (Above) President Truman sees at first hand the ruins of Berlin in 1945; with him is Secretary of State James Byrnes and Admiral William D. Leahy. (Below) President Hoover places a wreath on the tomb of the Unknown Soldier in Arlington, Virginia, symbol of all the Americans who have died in service to their country.

7

THE PRESIDENT'S
JOBS—III:

Head of State, of His Political Party and of the Nation's First Family

In addition to being chief Executive and commander in chief of the armed forces, the president is also the nation's ceremonial head of state, the head of the nation's first family and leader of his political party. While he is in the White House, the president and his family are closely watched by the communications media, and the people look to the White House for moral leadership and inspiration. The president is expected to lead the country not only in its affairs of state but in all walks of life.

(Above) President Hoover with his granddaughter, Peggy Ann, leaving Christ Episcopal Church in Alexandria, Virginia, in 1931; (facing page) President and Mrs. Eisenhower dressed for a state dinner at the Ethiopian Embassy, 1954.

(The Herbert Hoover Library)

President and Mrs. Hoover stop to talk with representatives of the Boy and Girl Scouts of America at the Governor's Mansion in Indianapolis (1931). *(The Herbert Hoover Library)*

The president and his family are expected to encourage the nation's cultural activities. (Below) President Kennedy congratulates cellist Pablo Casals after a special White House concert. Mrs. Kennedy is at Casals' right. *(The White House)*

One of the president's duties is to sign hundreds of proclamations every year—such as one proclaiming, "I am an American Day," May 19, 1940. President Roosevelt makes it official. *(The Franklin D. Roosevelt Library)*

President Johnson's concern with the housewife's problems was dramatized by his appointment of a Special Assistant for Consumer Affairs, former television personality Betty Furness (above). *(Y. R. Okamoto/ The Lyndon B. Johnson Library)*

The openings of monuments and public buildings of historical significance usually call for a presidential appearance. The president tries to attend as many of these events as his schedule will permit. (Above) President Hoover takes the first walk across the Lincoln Memorial Bridge in Washington, D.C., in 1932. (Left) President Truman speaks at the unveiling of a statue of George Washington, in 1950, at the Masonic Temple in Alexandria, Virginia. (Facing page) President Roosevelt attends the opening ceremonies on August 30, 1936, for the Mount Rushmore Memorial in South Dakota, designed by Gutzon Borglum.

(The Franklin D. Roosevelt Library)

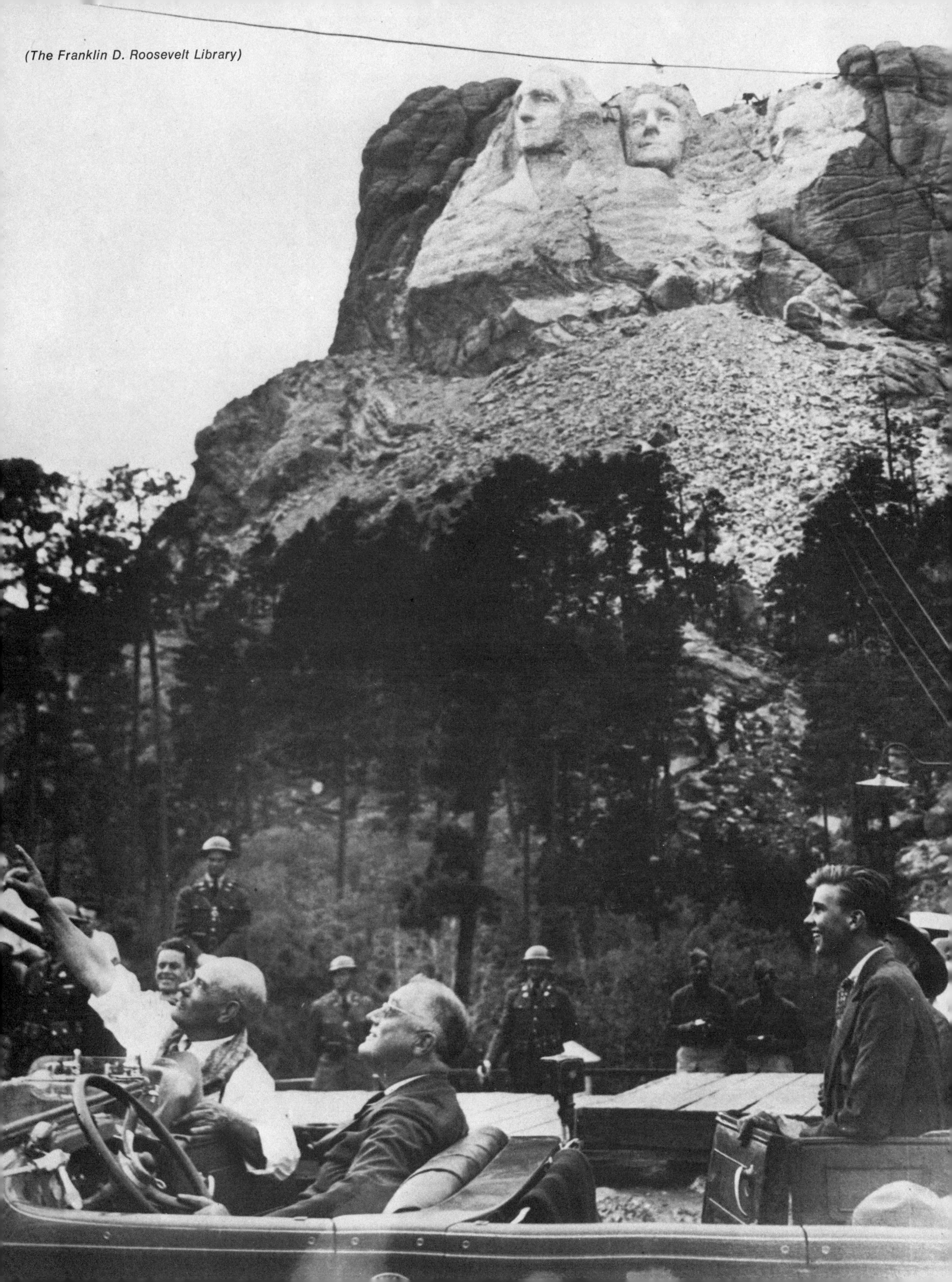

While the president tries to remain above partisan politics, he cannot ignore members of his political party who nominated and helped to elect him. Therefore, he must work closely with them. (Above) President Eisenhower talks politics in his White House Office, 1953, with chairman of the Republican National Committee Leonard Hall. (Below)

President Hoover attends a meeting with members of the Republican National Committee in 1931. "The President and Vice President," said Hoover, "are elected as the chosen leaders of a political party with declared mandates, principles, solutions of issues and promises to the people."

(Above) President Roosevelt (center) attends the 1938 Jefferson–Jackson Day Dinner, one of the party's annual fundraising functions. "I believe . . . it is my duty as the head of the Democratic Party," said Roosevelt, "to see to it that my party remains the truly liberal party in the political life of America." Most Republican presidents feel, similarly, that it is their obligation to maintain the Republican party as the conservative force in the country—although there are many Republicans who consider themselves "liberal" and many Democrats who consider themselves "conservative." *(The Franklin D. Roosevelt Library)*

Most presidents try to be elected for a second term. This requires the support of their political party. But their nomination is virtually certain. "When the President is sitting in the White House," said President Truman, "the National convention has never gone against his recommendations in the choice of a candidate . . . ," a situation that still exists. (Right) President Truman campaigns for reelection in 1948. *(Abbie Rowe/The Harry S. Truman Library)*

No matter where he is, the president of the United States is always on call. With so many duties and responsibilities, the presidency is a demanding, tiring job, but the president can never let up. However, it is essential that he stay in good health, which is a matter of concern to every citizen. The president is assigned a personal physician who is always on call and usually accompanies the president on long trips. It is his duty to see that the president gets proper rest, relaxation and exercise. (Left) President Kennedy takes a phone call at the airport in Detroit; (below) President Truman with his personal doctor, General Wallace Graham. (Facing page) Six presidents taking time out to relax.

(The John F. Kennedy Library)

(The Harry S. Truman Library)

(The John F. Kennedy Library)

(The Dwight D. Eisenhower Library)

(The Herbert Hoover Library)

(The Harry S. Truman Library)

(The Franklin D. Roosevelt Library)

(The Lyndon B. Johnson Library)

The president, like most Americans, tries to spend what spare time he has, his holidays and his vacation, with his family. (Above) President Eisenhower with his family on a 1954 vacation at Camp David, a presidential retreat maintained by the government in nearby Maryland. (Below) President Johnson lights the White House Christmas tree, a ceremony that launches the Christmas season for all Americans.

There are times, however, when the president just wants to be alone. *(The John F. Kennedy Library)*

8

FROM THE WHITE HOUSE INTO HISTORY:

The Presidential Libraries

One problem in recent years has been what to do with all the personal papers, documents, letters, and gifts a president accumulates while he is in office. Because the presidency was created by the Constitution, rather than the Congress or the federal government, it has been understood—since the presidency of George Washington—that the papers relating to his time in office are the president's private property and that he is free to take them with him when he leaves office and to dispose of them in any way he wishes. However, it is obvious that these papers have tremendous public value and that no really accurate history of a period can be written without access to the papers of the president who occupied the White House during that period.

Franklin Roosevelt was the first president to feel, while in office, the need of an organized method of preserving his presidential effects. To begin with, he was a born collector and had accumulated many papers, books and documents even before he entered the White House. Also, during the Roosevelt

administration, to a greater degree than ever before, Americans developed the habit of writing personal letters to the president—probably as a result of Roosevelt's warm personality and his "fireside chats," which combined to bring him closer to the people than any previous president. Therefore, in addition to the "official" papers, F.D.R. had hundreds of thousands of letters written by Americans in all walks of life. Finally, there was the problem of gifts. All presidents—and Roosevelt especially—receive thousands of gifts while they are in the

Model for the Presidential Libraries. The Rutherford B. Hayes Presidential Library in Fremont, Ohio. Functioning since 1916, it contains books, manuscripts, pamphlets, documents, 50,000 photographs of the Hayes era, and other memorabilia related to the life and presidency of Rutherford B. Hayes. The site, which includes the Hayes home, is operated by the Ohio Historical Society and the Hayes Foundation. *(Rutherford B. Hayes Presidential Library)*

White House. Some of them are very costly and it is not really appropriate to keep them. On the other hand, it is often difficult and, in the case of gifts from foreign rulers, undiplomatic, to return them. In Roosevelt's case, all these problems were compounded by the fact that he was in office longer than any other president, and had accumulated more material relating to his time in the White House than any previous president.

This prompted Roosevelt, in consultation with some of the nation's more distinguished scholars, to develop the idea of a combination library and museum to serve as a depository for all his letters, papers, documents, gifts and memorabilia accumulated while in office. It was recommended that it be modeled after the Rutherford B. Hayes Presidential Library in Fremont, Ohio. And it was decided that it would be built at Hyde Park, New York, where Roosevelt was born and raised. The land was donated to the government by his family and the money for constructing the buildings was raised through public donations. In return for this valuable and historically important donation, the federal government, under a joint congressional resolution passed in 1939, agreed to administer the library and provide a professional staff. This became the established procedure for developing all presidential libraries, and under the Presidential Libraries Act of 1955, library-museums have been created for Presidents Hoover, Truman, Eisenhower, Kennedy and Johnson. They are under the overall direction of the National Archives and Records Service of the General Services Administration.

The libraries have been eminently popular and successful. Every year, more than one-and-a-half-million people visit the six presidential libraries. Historians, scholars and authors have found them to be invaluable sources of documents, books and photographs. When a president leaves the White House, he inevitably passes into history, and the presidential libraries have helped provide this transition.

President Roosevelt dedicating the Franklin D. Roosevelt Library at Hyde Park in June 1941. "To bring together the records of the past," he said, "and to house them in buildings where they will be preserved for the use of men and women in the future, a Nation must believe in three things. It must believe in the past. It must believe in the future. It must, above all, believe in the capacity of its people to learn from the past so that they can gain in judgment in creating their own future." *(The Franklin D. Roosevelt Library)*

THE HERBERT HOOVER LIBRARY
WEST BRANCH, IOWA

Many of Herbert Hoover's presidential effects were originally housed at the Hoover Institution on War, Revolution and Peace at Stanford University. The papers relating to war relief still remain there. However, since 1962, the rest of Hoover's papers and memorabilia relating to his public service as secretary of commerce and as president, and to his long retirement are in the library (above) at West Branch, Iowa, where Hoover was born. The cottage in which he was born and other buildings in West Branch associated with Hoover have been restored. They are now administered by the National Park Service. President Hoover and his wife, Lou Henry, are buried at West Branch, which is just off Interstate 80, 120 miles east of Des Moines. *(The Herbert Hoover Library)*

Herbert Hoover and his grandchildren look at some of the library displays during the 1962 dedication. His son Allan Hoover and Allan's wife, Margaret, are at the right. *(The Herbert Hoover Library)*

THE FRANKLIN D. ROOSEVELT LIBRARY
HYDE PARK, NEW YORK

The Franklin D. Roosevelt Library is located at Hyde Park, New York, a few miles north of Poughkeepsie on Route 9. Also open to the public is the Roosevelt family home, which is adjacent to the library and administered by the National Park Service. (Roy Hoopes)

Included in the F.D.R. exhibits is the famous "sphinx," featured at the 1939 Gridiron dinner in Washington—inspired by President Roosevelt's prolonged silence on the question of whether he planned to seek reelection to an unprecedented third term in 1940. (The Franklin D. Roosevelt Library)

THE HARRY S. TRUMAN LIBRARY
INDEPENDENCE, MISSOURI

The Truman Library is in Independence, Missouri, on a knoll facing U.S. Highway 24. "This Library," said Truman, expressing an opinion that applies equally well to all presidential libraries, "will belong to the people of the United States. My papers will be the property of the people and be accessible to them. And this is as it should be. The papers of the President are among the most valuable sources of material for history. They ought to be preserved and they ought to be used." *(The Harry S. Truman Library)*

The libraries are designed not only as depositories and museums but as offices in which the former president can work on his memoirs and engage in whatever other activities he desires. (Above) President Truman and his former secretary of state, Dean Acheson, participate in a meeting of the Truman Library Institute. *(The Harry S. Truman Library)*

THE DWIGHT D. EISENHOWER LIBRARY
ABILENE, KANSAS

At the ground-breaking ceremonies for his library at Abilene, Kansas, President Eisenhower said: "When this library is filled with documents, and scholars come here to probe into some of the facts of the past half-century, I hope that they, as we today, are concerned primarily with ideals, principles and trends that provide guides to a free, rich, peaceful future in which all peoples can achieve ever rising levels of human well-being." *(The Dwight D. Eisenhower Library)*

In the stacks at the Eisenhower Library, archivists examine the millions of documents, such as General Eisenhower's "Assumption of Command" of the European Forces in 1944 (below), stored in containers that line the walls of the library "stacks." Also at the Eisenhower Center is the Eisenhower Museum, the Eisenhower family home, and the Place of Meditation, the final resting place of President Eisenhower and his first son, Doud Dwight. *(The Dwight D. Eisenhower Library)*

General Eisenhower

~~R E S T R I C T E D~~

Hq ETOUSA   16 January 1944

ASSUMPTION OF COMMAND

By direction of the President, I assume command of the European er of Operations, effective this date.

Dwight D Eisenhower
DWIGHT D. EISENHOWER
General, United States Army
Commanding.

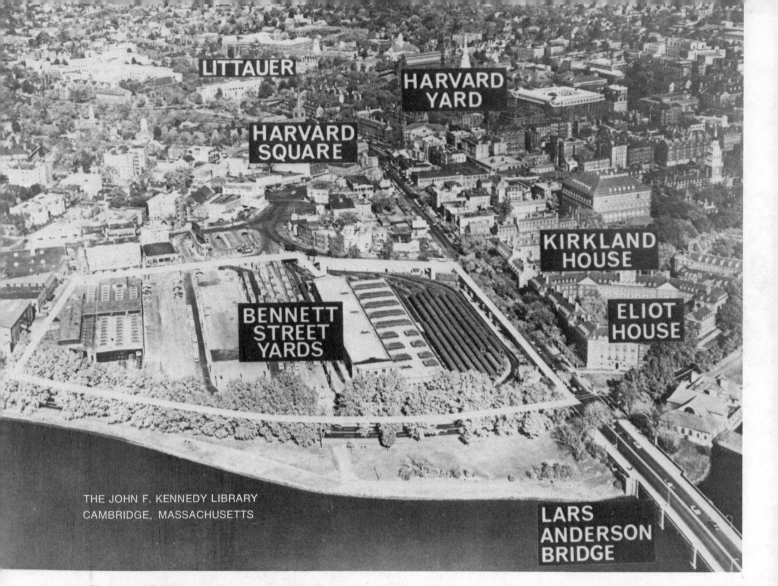

THE JOHN F. KENNEDY LIBRARY
CAMBRIDGE, MASSACHUSETTS

The John F. Kennedy Library, with its vast collection of documents, papers, photographs and unique oral history tapes, is temporarily functioning in the Federal Archives and Records Center at Waltham, Massachusetts. However, plans are underway for the construction of a permanent building on the Bennett Street yards site at Memorial Drive and Boylston Street in Cambridge, Massachusetts.

It overlooks the Charles River and is near the Harvard Square and Yard, where John Kennedy spent his university days. Also located on this site will be a museum, and the Kennedy School of Government and Institute of Politics of Harvard University. *(The John F. Kennedy Library)*

At the John F. Kennedy Building in Boston, Mass., Senator Edward M. Kennedy (D–Mass.), younger brother of the late President Kennedy, studies a photo exhibit. *(The John F. Kennedy Library)*

THE LYNDON B. JOHNSON LIBRARY
AUSTIN, TEXAS

The Lyndon B. Johnson Library is on the University of Texas campus, in Austin, just west of the Memorial Stadium Exit on Interstate 35. "I hope that visitors who come here," said Johnson, "will achieve a closer understanding of the office of the Presidency, which affects their own lives so greatly. I hope that those who shared in the history of this time will remember it and see it in perspective, and that the young people who come here will get a clearer comprehension of what this Nation tried to do in an eventful period in its history." (The Lyndon B. Johnson Library)

School children studying the LBJ Biography Case at the Lyndon B. Johnson Library in Austin. (The Lyndon B. Johnson Library)

9

"...TRUST WITH POWER THAT APPALLS A THINKING MAN...."

The office of the presidency combines the royal duties of a monarch and the political power of an elected leader. "A King and Prime Minister rolled into one," as President Theodore Roosevelt put it. "The American President not only reigns," says historian Sidney Hyman, "he also rules."

To be a king and a prime minister at the same time is a tremendous responsibility. And perhaps the ultimate test of how well a president does his job is his ability to reconcile the various interests in national policy disputes in which two or more groups have legitimate, but conflicting, demands. Some presidents have thrived on the job; others have found it too much of a burden for one man. But all agree that there is no experience in life that can prepare a man for the presidency, and the only way to comprehend the complexity and demands of this distinguished office is to serve in it.

"The President of the United States is obliged to determine a multitude of questions and policies. By the Constitution he must recommend to Congress such measures as he shall deem necessary and expedient, and he is required to finally pass upon every act of Congress. He is the Chief Executive of the greatest business in the world, which at some point touches upon every single activity of our people.

"By his position he must, within his capacities, give leadership to the development of moral, social, and economic forces outside of government which make for betterment of our country."—Herbert Hoover *(The Herbert Hoover Library)*

124

"You will recognize, I think, that a true function of the head of the Government of the United States is to find among many discordant elements that unity of purpose that is best for the Nation as a whole. This is necessary because government is not merely one of the many coordinate groups in the community or the Nation, but government is essentially the outward expression of the unity and the leadership of all groups."—Franklin D. Roosevelt *(The Franklin D. Roosevelt Library)*

"The Constitution states that 'the executive power shall be vested in a President of the United States of America.' These words put a tremendous responsibility on the individual who happens to be President. He holds an office of immense power. It surely is the greatest trust that can be placed in any man by the American people. It is trust with a power that appalls a thinking man. There have been men in history who have liked power and the glamour that goes with it: Alexander, Caesar, Napoleon, to name only a few. I never did. It was only the responsibility that I felt to the people who had given me this power that concerned me. I believe that the power of the President should be used in the interest of the people, and in order to do that the President must use whatever power the Constitution does not expressly deny him."—Harry S. Truman *(The Harry S. Truman Library)*

"To this office—to the President, whoever he may be, there comes every day from all parts of the land and from all parts of the world a steady flow of dispatches, reports and visitors. They tell of the successes and the disappointments of our people in their efforts to help achieve peace with justice in the world. They tell, too, of the progress and difficulties in building a sturdy, prosperous and a just society here at home.

"On the basis of this information, decisions, affecting all of us, have to be made every day. Because your President, aside from the Vice President, is the only governmental official chosen by a vote of all the people, he must make his decisions on the basis of what he thinks best for all the people. He cannot consider only a district, a state or a region in developing solutions to problems. He must always use the yardstick of the national interest."—Dwight D. Eisenhower (*The Dwight D. Eisenhower Library*)

"There is no experience you can get that possibly can prepare you adequately for the Presidency. . . . When I ran for the Presidency I knew this country faced serious challenges, but I could not realize—nor could any man realize who does not bear the burden of the office—how heavy and constant would be those burdens."—John F. Kennedy (*The John F. Kennedy Library*)

126

"The magnitude of the job dwarfs every man who aspires to it. Every man who occupies the position has to strain to the utmost of his ability to fill it. I believe that every man who ever occupied it, within his inner self, was humble enough to realize that no living mortal has ever possessed all the required qualifications. It is not a question of the incumbents' wanting to do the right thing. The American people, in their wisdom, have never yet elected an evil man to lead them. No man ever runs for the Presidency on a platform of doing wrong. Every President wants earnestly to do what is right. The enormous challenge he faces, as he looks out on his country and the world from the observation post of the White House, is knowing what is the right thing to do, for the complexities of the problems are past description."—Lyndon B. Johnson (*The Lyndon B. Johnson Library*)

Other Presidential Sites
of Historic Interest

Rutherford B. Hayes
Presidential Library
Fremont, Ohio

Abraham Lincoln's Home
Lincoln City, Illinois

Andrew Jackson's Home
The Hermitage
Tennessee

William Howard Taft
Birthplace and Home
Cincinnati, Ohio

Theodore Roosevelt
Home and Museum
Sagamore Hill
Oyster Bay, L.I., New York

George Washington's Home
Mount Vernon
Alexandria, Virginia

Adams Family National
Historic Site
Quincy, Massachusetts